Breaking Up with my Wheelchair

By Kelly-Anne Kerley

Breaking Up With My Wheelchair

Copyright © 2024 Kelly-Anne Kerley

First published 2024

Published by Disruptive Publishing

    17 Spencer Avenue
    Deception Bay QLD 4508
    Australia
    www.disruptivepublishing.com.au

Book cover design by Andy Cooke: www.andycooke.work

Front cover image by Brad Amos:

bradamos.com and instagram.com/bradamos_photography

 Thank you to BLACK SHEEP for supplying the kit I'm wearing on the front cover. #lovewomenscycling

All Rights Reserved. No part of this publication may be reproduced, distributed or transmitted in any form, or by any means, including photocopying, recording, or any other electronic methods, without the prior written permission of the publishers. Brief quotations that are credited to the publication and the author are permitted.

ISBN Print: 978-1-7636156-6-3
ISBN Ebook: 978-1-7636156-7-0

Working with Kelly-Anne on her journey back to bike riding has been incredibly inspiring. Her determination and resilience in overcoming the challenges posed by her spinal cord injury are nothing short of remarkable. Through our recreation therapy sessions, I witnessed firsthand her progress and unwavering spirit, which ultimately culminated in the achievement of her goal—to get back on her bike. Her book beautifully captures this journey, offering profound insights and encouragement to others facing similar challenges. I highly recommend it as a testament to the power of perseverance and the transformative impact of recreation therapy in rehabilitation.

~ **Amanda Vizas**
Senior Recreation Therapist, Brain and Spinal Injury Rehabilitation

Kelly-Anne's book is a testament to the human spirit of survival and *thrival*. This is a powerful, inspirational, and encouraging book on not just overcoming adversity but flourishing beyond it. Her strong statements and regular reflections add a touch of humour and power to the story. Explaining your 'why it is what has driven me: wanting to capture my story—inclusive of my struggles, heartache, key learnings and, of course, achievements—to provide hope for others'.
You have written the book on transforming anxiety into action and positivity. Your beautiful humanness is expressed in your concern for your parents.
I would recommend and encourage anyone to read this book as it is an epic story of recovery.

~ **Di Riddell**
Speaker, Confidence Coach, and Author of *Speak Out*
www.diriddell.com

To my mother, my friend, Lorraine.
Thank you for your unwavering strength, support,
and constant listening ear.
For loving me always, for holding my hand,
and for cheering me on.

And for anyone brave enough to believe they can,
a mother's love will help guide you.

Recognise that, if you try, there is always hope.

Table of Contents

Foreword 9
PART ONE: Hospital 11
I Got Hit By A Car! 13
Waking Up 17
Surgery And More Surgery 19
Waking Up Again 21
Life In The Spinal Cord Ward 27
Ho-Hum Days On Spinal Cord Ward E 33
My Hero Skills 37
Birthday Steps 43
Reality Bites 47
Changing Hospitals 51
Mum's Back!! And I'm On The Move Again 55
Breaking Up With My Wheelchair 61
Goal Posts Shift— Time To Pivot 67
Trial Sleep-Overs 73
PART TWO: Home 81
Home Time—Three Months And One Day 83
Building My New-Normal Life 87
That Morning: Piecing Things Together 95
Talking To The Police 97
Back On The Bike 101
My First Fall 109

Returning To Adelaide And Visiting Mum 113
Travelling Solo 117
PART THREE: Hero Skills 119
Meeting A Fellow Paraplegic 121
Who Am I: Struggling With My Identity 125
OMG!! First Anniversary Already 135
Returning To Work 139
The Elusive 100km! 143
Second Anniversary: #dowhatyoulove 147
Kicking Goals 153
Where Am I Now? 159
About The Author 163
Acknowledgements 165
Contact Kelly-Anne 169
Resources 171

Foreword

In May 2021, I reconnected with Kelly-Anne for lunch after learning about her cycling accident, which resulted in a spinal cord injury. I'm often asked to connect with individuals who have sustained such injuries, and provided they are ready and willing to discuss their 'new normal,' it is a privilege to support and encourage them through such a transformative experience.

Seeing Kelly-Anne sitting at a table without a wheelchair was a special moment. Her grit and determination to progress so far after such devastating injuries is truly admirable.

After a spinal cord injury, it's easy to stop and give up, to say, "I can't, it's not worth it, leave me alone." The alternative involves hard work, both physically and mentally, but the rewards can build resilience and fuel persistence and determination, ultimately leading to a fulfilling life, albeit one that may be unimagined.

Kelly-Anne's story exemplifies the true essence of potential through adversity. She had the courage to forge a path forward, face her fears, and move past them, setting herself up for a future full of possibility and providing inspiration for others at the crossroads of spinal cord injury.

Breaking Up with my Wheelchair offers readers a chance to reflect and consider. Possibilities surround all of us, but only those who seize the opportunities reap the rewards.

John Maclean
Motivational Speaker, Author and Paralympian

PART ONE: Hospital

I Got Hit By A Car!

True story.

One driver's single moment of inattention … and my life changed forever.

It was May 13, 2020, I was cycling one minute and the next minute I was waking up in ICU (Intensive Care Unit) completely unaware of why I was there, or that I'd had to have multiple surgeries to keep me alive.

Let me tell you about it.

An avid cyclist, I would often set out early to ride around Sydney, enjoy a morning of exercise, and meet friends—thriving on the adrenaline and rush of pedaling outside in the fresh air. The sport I love, with many adventures out on the open road.

Amidst the Covid-19 pandemic there were a lot of restrictions, cycling in groups being one of them. Limited to pairs, my friend Jacqui and I set out on our bikes early—the destination Manly—to catch up, enjoy a coffee, and to watch the sunrise.

I never saw the sunrise that day.

Whilst rolling through the traffic lights on the boulevard I was hit by a car, the driver had failed to give way. Their single moment of inattention literally changed the course of my life.

It's now three years post-accident and it's time for me to share my story with you. It's real, it's raw and it's heartfelt, and I hope you get something from me being vulnerable enough to share it. What follows is my extraordinary journey from being completely incapacitated to learning to walk—and ride—again. It's an immense journey of pain and loss and recovery, and a lot has happened, but every step of the way there have been wins, big and small, including many learning experiences.

It's an open and honest account of hospital life interwoven with my Mum's account of what was happening, as recorded in her personal diary of events.

These include her personal struggles, my hospital care and rehabilitation, her thoughts about the constant adjustments to life post-hospital, and her observations of me learning to live with life-changing injuries.

I wanted to write this book for me, but I also wanted it to be a tribute to my amazing Mother, my support network and my cheerleaders, and to inspire you, the reader.

Nurturing and coaching come naturally to me, hence, after my life-changing experience I felt the need to share what I went through—and continue to go through—so that I can help other people.

I wanted to share how every part of the experience has woven together leading to immense personal growth as I build my 'new normal'.

My transformation and newfound look on life hasn't come easily. It's still difficult, but I hope my story will help others—whether they are coping with trauma or supporting a loved one—through changing their dialogue, their mindset, their thinking, and their negative language to be healthier and more positive in order to improve their mental wellness.

Providing inspiration and encouragement to look forward and not give up—that's powerful for me. Clearly it wasn't my time, and it has taken me a while to realise that having a meaningful and powerful voice is my new purpose, but it feels right. It's a nice feeling to think I can make a positive difference, and although my accident and injuries don't define me, they now form an important part of who I am. My WHY. 😊

Living with an incomplete Spinal Cord Injury (SCI), and a Traumatic Brain Injury (TBI) amongst other injuries, I'm proud I chose to believe in me. I did the hard work, I changed my thinking, and through this process I turned hope*less* into hope*ful*.

I don't remember seeing the car, feeling the impact of the collision, or anything else that happened until I woke up in ICU six days after the accident.

This is where my story begins …

Waking Up

Groggy, unaware of my surroundings, I'm unable to communicate. What is this thing obstructing my throat? I become quite panicked. I soon realise I can't move; nor can I feel my arms or legs. What's going on? I quickly become disoriented, confusion consuming me. Surrounded by multiple cords connected to machines, I'm further baffled seeing my terribly distraught mother in the corner of the room.

What is she doing here? She lives in Adelaide. Why is she in Sydney? Where am I? What's happening?

Seeing tears of grief and sadness in my mother's eyes disturbs me immensely, and without the ability to communicate I can't fathom what is happening. I try to grunt until a gentle hand touches my shoulder, I can only assume to try and calm me. What *is* this thing obstructing my throat?! Breathing is such a struggle and I feel like I'm choking. Although I can have no understanding of it at this point, I have been 'intubated': a tube has been inserted through my mouth down into my trachea, artificially keeping my airway open.

A word board is put in front of me, which I vaguely get the sense is to help with communicating, however, with one eye quite swollen, I struggle to blink or raise my eyebrows to identify letters or words. Drained, I give up.

Unbeknown to me, I have sustained multiple traumatic injuries to my face, ribs, and cervical spine. Having already undergone two major surgeries on my spine, I am in a critical condition and a particularly fragile state.

The nurse mentions something about surgery and that Mum will be back tomorrow. I've no real comprehension of what any of this means. Moaning, and in a lot of pain, I receive an injection in my abdomen. Cloudy confusion sweeps over me, the disturbed and saddened vision of my Mum causes tears to roll down my own cheeks. I close my eyes, exhausted, and drift off.

Surgery And More Surgery

I'm sent back into surgery to fix my broken jaw, and with major concern around my ability to breathe on my own, the potential of a tracheotomy is real. I'm weak, having lost a lot of weight and muscle over the past six days. Poor Mum, more life-changing decisions to be made. With her heart breaking, she must sign papers giving permission to make a hole in my throat—should the need arise.

After seven long hours Mum receives a call that the surgery has gone well. Relief washes over her as she learns there was no need for her little girl to have a tracheotomy.

Later, I learn that my jaw was *so* broken that the majority of the surgery was completed through the roof of my mouth. From the surgeon's perspective this was a good thing, as I required only one tiny incision below my right cheek. With my face finally cleaned up I'm left with stitches in my chin—cut deeply from the impact of hitting the car's windscreen face-first—and in the corner of my right eye where my sunglasses broke into my face.

Two metal rods and ten screws now form a permanent fixture in my neck, with another five metal plates in my face. Unable to move my arms or legs, a neck brace protects my fragile spine. Unaware of the enormity or severity of my injuries, I remain in ICU for a further five days.

Waking Up Again

Upon waking in strange surroundings, I'm groggy and disoriented, and tears roll down my cheeks. Seeing Mum is comforting, yet worrying, as I remain numb all over, still not comprehending what is happening. I can finally speak a little, albeit with difficulty, with my mouth held closed by bands over screws in both my top and bottom jawbone. Nothing makes sense as I struggle to share what's going on for me.

* * *

Reflection: I would love to share more with you about the moment I woke up, and the events of the preceding weeks, however, I have no recollection of any of it.

* * *

My mother, however, kept a diary during this time, which I'm grateful for. Here is what she wrote:

How do I be strong for my girl?

I'm her Mum, I need to fix her …

Today I sat and brushed her hair, performed some exercises moving her wrists and fingers, as directed by the nurses, and was told to be brave. How? I'm scared I will bruise her, and I'm fearful of making the wrong decisions.

* * *

Reflection: I truly believe, to this day, that this fogginess was my brain protecting me and helping me to remain calm.

* * *

A nurse comes into ICU introducing herself as a 'breathing physio'. What's that?

Small, yet strong hands cup either side of my ribs applying pressure with a pump-like motion as I am forced to cough. I'm told to spit and cough repeatedly, a test, as I learn how to breathe again. Tedious and extremely painful, it's repeated twice daily whilst I'm lying down, *still* unable to move. Discovering I have a cracked top rib is not providing any joy in this exercise. An elastic brace is an uncomfortable addition, forming a compression-like binder around my ribs, similar to a corset. I'm told this will help support my abdomen, maintain pressure, and help improve my respiratory function.

My neck brace rubs and irritates me, yet it is necessary to support my fragile spine whilst it heals after my surgeries. Stuck lying on my back I'm unable to move, I strain to see what's going on around me. Soon, changing into a smaller, kid's neck brace provides only minimal relief.

The left side of my mouth droops and is quite numb from a deep cut to my chin which is impacting the surrounding nerves. Screws and bands hold my jaw in place restricting my diet to liquids. With my weight still dropping, the nurses introduce jelly. Hello, mandarin-flavoured goodness, OMG, the best thing ever! Sweet, cool, and delicious, not to mention soothing for my throat as it slides down. I'm sure I have a smile on my face—albeit a crooked one. I know Mum is probably smiling too, as I've never particularly liked jelly.

I'm instructed to cough several times a day, but it is difficult, painful, and quite tiring. It's a must to clear my lungs of phlegm, demonstrating that things are beginning to function again. Mum is constantly by my side helping where she can. Today she's helping with the suction, that's not something a mum should have to do. That I have to see my Mum look after me like a baby upsets me. Yet deep down I know she wouldn't be anywhere else.

My father and boyfriend aren't permitted into ICU due to Covid-19 restrictions, so Facetime is organised. I vaguely recall seeing their faces yet, sadly, I've no recollection of what was said, or the feelings felt.

I'm further diagnosed with a Traumatic Brain Injury (TBI), a result of the impact of the crash and going face-first into the car's windscreen. I have blanks in my memory that cause me additional frustrations.

* * *

Reflection: To this day, trying to remember even the first wiggle of my toes sadly draws a blank for me.

A lot of activities take place within ICU that I don't recall, however, I'm sure I owe a lot of my healing and movement to my mother's diligent bedside manner.

* * *

I'm introduced to an Occupational Therapist (OT), and splints are fitted on my hands. Mum is shown multiple exercises to help release built-up fluid in my fingers in the hope I'll get some feeling and movement return to them.

Mum's Diary Note: Hope this better bloody works.

Reflection: To this day she reminds me of how much time she spent by my bedside, massaging my hands, and talking to me. I listen and smile, grateful I have such a loving mother.

* * *

Another nurse asks me multiple questions: what's my date of birth, what day is it, what hospital am I in, is it morning or night? How annoying, as I can't understand why I'm being asked. There is a large clock within my room in ICU displaying date, weekday, and time. Mum smiles at me as she soon realises I'm glancing over at the clock. I giggle.

Next, a series of pictures is shown to me, which I don't pay any attention to because they don't appear to have any relevance. The next morning when I'm asked about the pictures, which I don't recall, it's revealed to me they're testing my memory—post-traumatic amnesia tests due to the knock to my head.

Ahh, okay people, well it helps if you share *why*. I'm sure I roll my eyes. I try to remember them for the next day.

A few more laughs follow as I discover I have medical tape quite high on my inner thigh, which is seriously itchy. I ask Mum to scratch it, and Mum jokes my boyfriend should be here. We both laugh which feels so good after the traumatic events of the past few days.

Mum's Diary Note: Starting to look like my girl, swelling going down. Smart chick looking at the clock to answer daily cognitive challenges. So good to have a laugh and feel a sense of my girl's personality shining through.

I spend a total of eleven days in ICU.

Waking Up Again

My life as I know it has changed FOREVER. My fight to survive and rebuild is only just beginning.

Life In The Spinal Cord Ward

I thank the nurses within ICU who diligently sat in the cubicle outside my room twenty-four hours a day for the past eleven days. I'm now being transferred to the Spinal Cord Ward 7th Floor, Ward E, Bed 12, surrounded by the ugliest orange and white striped curtains. I'm left here feeling lonely, scared, and claustrophobic.

It's my first night out of ICU, my jaw begins to ache and becomes excruciatingly painful. I cry and moan out loud for what feels like hours as the nurse tries to contact a night doctor to approve further pain medication. The nurse tries to comfort me by tenderly stroking my forehead, pain clearly showing all over my sweaty, anguished face as what felt like hours passed. Never have I experienced such intense pain.

Finally, I'm prescribed maximum pain killers, and eventually I find peace as I pass out. I'm thankful for the caring nurse as the reality of my injuries sets in and becomes all-too real.

Orange and white coloured curtains, with an odd green stripe, become my new surroundings. As if being bed-bound isn't challenging enough, I am now starved of natural light. This is tough for me mentally, and I repeatedly ask the nurses to leave my front curtain open.

Breaking Up With My Wheelchair

Breakfast, usually my favourite meal of the day, isn't so enjoyable here: soggy porridge fed to me like an infant, inclusive of spills down my chin has me feeling quite degraded. I'm left with a sense of helplessness. I must constantly ask for help, even for a sip of water.

It's time for my first shower in twelve days. I need to be hoisted out of bed, as I am unable to move, into a special chair for toileting and showering. I'm speechless as the nurses fuss over me moving my limbs into the harness. Slowly the harness scoops me up, what an odd feeling. Still in a gown, the nurse undresses, washes, and dries me. At forty-one years of age my independence has gone; I feel so vulnerable as immense sadness takes over.

Mum's Diary Note: Using a hoist to transfer her in and out of bed, so heartbreaking to watch Kelly, it's not fair. How do I watch her every day do this? Please give me strength.

My neck brace rubs on my skin causing constant discomfort, and I feel immense relief when it's removed and replaced with a separate one for showering. The brace around my ribs is also removed for showering. Such a mission every morning, it feels like Groundhog Day! I just want to do it myself; my own body feels foreign to me, my limbs are like a puppet on a string.

Mum brings me in some clothes, storing them in two tiny bedside drawers. Tops needing to be stretched over my head and neck brace, tracksuit pants roomy enough to allow for my catheter, so hideous and uncomfortable.

Underwear optional ... what was the point? I can't manage either a bra or underpants. Even putting deodorant and moisturiser on is a luxury. I'm thankful for Mum as she does so much for me, including washing my clothes and charging my phone. I find it difficult to sleep with only curtains separating me from other patients, all with their own challenges and varying levels of spinal cord injuries. Noises, cries of pain ... I don't even want to know what's causing them.

I'm so grateful for Mum's daily support and patience with me, she's almost my shadow—just like at sport when I was young: constantly cheering me on.

Whilst I was in ICU I was measured for my manual wheelchair, which now turns up. Hoisted out of bed into the wheelchair, I can now attend physio sessions. Physios come onto the ward every morning and introduce themselves, encouraging patients to attend. Physio is available twice a day, Monday to Friday. I go every day, ten times a week, voluntarily, but I'm committed to rebuilding. These activities are exhausting, I'm easily frustrated giving all my energy and effort, applying myself at the exercises and constantly wondering why my legs, hands, and arms won't move like they used to. I feel so powerless.

Now my arms are tied up like a puppet. I'm connected to a pulley trying to mobilise my arms. It's embarrassing and painful, and my arms are numb and stinging, feelings of despair wash over me.

I'm constantly woken up throughout the night by nurses, turning me on my side to check for pressure wounds because I either sit or lay all day. Fortunately for me I have good skin. Well, so I'm told by one nurse who—after a few nights of checking my skin and providing the all-clear—gives me a cheeky, yet friendly, smack on my bottom. Mum and I laugh out aloud together, it was so funny and unexpected. It feels good to have a light-hearted moment and to see Mum's face relax, even temporarily.

It's now been over two weeks since my crash and I finally get to go and see my Dad and boyfriend. Having received permission to venture off the ward, I head downstairs in my wheelchair. Feels good, sense of progress. Mum and I receive education on the importance of emptying my catheter and looking out for signs of *autonomic dysreflexia*. It's an abnormal, overreaction of the involuntary nervous system to stimulation, and symptoms include a change in heart rate, excessive sweating or high blood pressure. It's heartbreaking having to rely on my Mum to empty my wee bag. She shouldn't have to do this. My excitement to get off of the ward and see my Dad and boyfriend overtakes these feelings.

My Dad, with his own medical problems, is here for Mum. I'm proud of him for showing up for her, he's so supportive and patiently waits each and every day whilst she is upstairs with me. My boyfriend's hand covers mine bringing tears to my eyes, emotions unable to be controlled. We sit, me numb and him not saying too much.

My food selection is 'soft' due to restrictions with my jaw, and it is dry, tasteless, and unappetising.

Protein smoothies and homemade vegetable soup are brought in to support my nutrition as I'm still not gaining weight. It's embarrassing having to ask loved ones to feed me or to hold my straw, but the need for sustenance and being comfortable with my loved ones overtakes this feeling. Usually a health fanatic, I take this opportunity to indulge in, and enjoy, biscuits. I don't hesitate after a morning of physio, joining Dad at lunchtime sharing his coffee, with biscuits being dunked, softening them the right amount for me to enjoy. Delicious.

Dad, his usual cheeky self, asks for an allowance to fund future coffees and his new-found enjoyment of Bakers Delight buns. How can I deprive him of these simple treats? Parents, hey!

Life In The Spinal Cord Ward

Back on the ward, an IT person attaches a stretchy arm onto my wheelchair, at the end is a Velcro round which adheres to the back of my phone. I'm shown how to use Siri and manage texts and emails with voice control. Although it's quite cool technology, it soon becomes just another frustrating thing I must navigate without the use of my hands. I've a lot of messages and voicemails, and I don't know where to start. All a bit overwhelming as it's not as simple as pressing buttons. It's frustratingly slow and cumbersome, with translation of voice-to-message riddled with errors. Grrr!

I'm pleased I can say, "Hey, Siri, call Mum," which works. Even after spending most of the day together, we often talk at night. It's comforting, as I am so lonely, and she is my only real connection to the outside world as my first few weeks in hospital slowly go by.

The next morning the nurses share that they are opening the ward next door, so all the female patients will be moved into it. Happiness washes over me as I'm given the bed near the window. Hello, natural light. 😊

Ho-Hum Days On Spinal Cord Ward E

I've a lot of time to think, however, I still struggle to comprehend the enormity of what is happening to me. And yet I'm acutely aware of what I'm putting my parents through, day after day. For me it's the constant mental and physical battle to keep going, its exhaustive and depressing. I'm moody, my usually cheery demeanour is absent.

My daily routine, Monday-to-Friday, sees the arrival of my breakfast followed by a nurse coming in to feed me, blood pressure reviewed, medication dispensed and taken, I'm showered, physio, lunch with my parents, usually physio again and rest. Exhausted.

I get a little bit savvy and cheeky this particular morning, it's been a few weeks now, and I find my sense of humour asking the nurse to heat up the milk to make my porridge soggy. I ask for my straw and proceed to drink my porridge, no mess on my face. I'm pretty pleased with myself—there's always a way, people! Lol!

My bladder and bowels are affected as a result of the damage to my spinal cord. Fortunately for me I have some sensation, yet they are still neurogenic, often causing a sense of urgency I am unable to control, just something else I must manage. With several embarrassing accidents I'm reassured it's quite normal, sadly it's another thing leaving me feeling incapable, sad, and disheartened.

I try to think that nurses deal with this kind of thing every day, but it's difficult if you've had an 'accident'. I am kindly reminded of this as one morning, during my ritual of being left in the bathroom awaiting my 'movement' while listening to Smooth FM on the radio, a nurse asks me if I'd like a cup of tea. Hot drinks help, apparently. "Seriously?" I ask. Nurse says, "Yes". Amazing, so I sit and enjoy my cuppa and listen to Smooth FM. I start the day off smiling and giggling as I tell the story to my bestie Carla. Love a bit of Smooth FM. LOL.

Shower, into my wheelchair, and off to physio I go, pleased with myself that's for sure. Getting on with things and doing my best in a difficult situation.

Mum often shows up as I finish physio, she joins in today as I have now progressed to standing and doing some squats supported by ballet bars. Lucky me having her so present.

Focusing on any and all positives, I'm delighted to be fitted for an electric wheelchair. I'm shown how to manoeuvre it, and I can just manage the steering knob as my left side slowly regains some sensation.

Tested on my handling skills through the halls of the ward, I accidently run over Mum's toes, yikes.

I have a sense of happiness and achievement as I begin to regain some movement and do things for myself. I'm warned to go cautiously as I'm still terribly weak.

Ho-Hum Days On Spinal Cord Ward E

Mum's Diary Note: Watch out people, she has wheels!

A senior doctor comes to the ward and Mum and I listen intently to what he has to say, with me craving information about what is happening to me, future rehab, and timeframes around healing. It is still early days as I'm told my body needs a *lot* of time to heal, not to mention a lot of rehabilitation activities.

I'm not the most patient of people, but I appreciate I just have to do what I am told and trust the process. What choice do I really have? None.

My days are mentally and physically draining: attending physio twice a day, heading downstairs to see my Dad, often quickly downing my protein shake, and then going back upstairs for Occupational Therapy.

I don't even make it downstairs today as I'm whisked away, still in my bed, as I am prone to 'dopplers' and they want to run the ultrasound over my legs. This is when you have blood clots and need to be constantly scanned to see if they've moved, as the doctors don't want them making their way to my heart. Knee-high compression socks, to support circulation, are worn most nights and often during the day due to my reduced movement. I'm learning so much more about what's happening to me. Education makes me feel better, understanding *what* is happening and *why*, helps alleviate the frustrations. Given the all-clear I'm wheeled back to the ward.

Having had the stitch in my right eye removed, my eyes are next to be tested. Who knew there are so many tiny fibres and nerve endings in our cheeks? Let's hope I haven't damaged any. I sigh with relief when I'm cleared of any immediate damage. But with my body undergoing enormous amounts of changes and healing, I will need to have my eyesight rechecked at some point in the future.

Reflection: What happened to me was quite surreal, and I feel as though I went through the motions day after day and did my best to understand, and get on with, all of the various therapies. I succumbed to hospital life, yet I remained as informed as I could by asking a lot of questions. Fortunately, that's how I usually operate and I'm sure the TBI protected me from many things. These days I suffer from anxiety over the smallest things; using breathing techniques and moving slowly through activities helps me to live as normal a life as I can. *#Bekindtoyourself*

My Hero Skills

I'm told I have a cracked tooth and, having been a dental nurse in a previous life, I push for it to be fixed sooner rather than later as there's a possibility the nerve is exposed. Last thing I need is more pain! Soon after, I am whisked away for an x-ray, more waiting around and, of course, it's at an inconvenient time. So annoying to miss out on physio, yet I'm pleased I am successful in my request to have my cracked tooth looked at.

The hospital dentist advises that a temporary fix will suffice until I can see my own dentist, as I will likely require a crown. Urgh! Sigh. As if my mouth isn't bad enough already.

Reflection: First signs of me driving my rehab, subconsciously my Hero Skills are kicking in. *#celebratewins*

Using my phone becomes easier, and it feels so good to be back in touch with the outside world. Friends begin to visit, which I co-ordinate with my lunch breaks downstairs.

It is quite touching to have people I work with visit. Although they are friends, it's a different kind of bond and friendship than those I'm closest to outside of work.

The constant variety of people visiting me, reaching out with supportive messages, plays a huge role in helping me stay focused and keeping my spirits up. My love of biscuits soon becomes common knowledge as visitors bring baked goodies. Arriving back at my bed one afternoon I find a container of homemade choc chip cookies with a note. One of my friends, Alex, has taken the liberty of sneaking onto the ward to see me, hilarious. Love her style and rockstar moves. Makes me smile for the rest of the day, and makes the nurses smile too as I share the story over and over.

Spinal Cord ward is noisy, sadly most patients are in pain, some much worse than me. Mum talks to the other patients and their partners, however, for me I find it too difficult. I have no desire to talk to people outside of the nurses and therapists. I'm never rude, but I have enough to deal with and my focus is on myself. At my request Mum brings in my noise-cancelling headphones as I'm craving the peace to sleep. I rely on Mum to charge them and put them on me when tucking me in at night, as my hand function is still limited. Nurses help me into my pyjamas, clean my teeth, and tuck me in if Mum isn't there. A pillow propped up at the end of my bed, so my feet don't droop, so many things. A priority to have the buzzer close to the side of my arm to alert the nurses if I need anything throughout the night.

It's the weekend, a glorious looking day, craving fresh air and the sun on my face I beg Mum to let me go outside. It's so nice to sit and chat to my friends, leaving the worries of rehab back on the ward.

Reflection: Sadly, I don't recall the first time I speak to Jacqui, or the words exchanged. I do know she's okay and I'm thankful she's a regular visitor as her infectious, bubbly self. 😊

Mum's Diary Note: Had my first hug today from Kelly standing up, felt so good. Physio is going well; she is doing so well. Brings tears to my eyes each day.

I'm thankful for my attentiveness, even though I'm constantly fighting fatigue I realise I have been given the wrong medication.

My Hero Skills

I am flabbergasted that this can happen, but so proud of myself for checking and asking. My awareness and curiosity of my surroundings is enhanced as I begin to feel better day-by-day. I keep the nurses on their toes asking for my catheter to be emptied, especially first thing in the morning. Throughout the day it gets heavy, and it's dangerous as urine can circulate back into my body and cause infection.

A social worker visits us downstairs multiple times over the week as there is a lot of paperwork to complete to ensure my medical bills are covered through Compulsory Third Party (CTP) insurance and iCare. (iCare offers services that aim to support and improve the quality of life for those recovering from serious accidents.) I'm not really across any of this, thankfully Mum is. She signs on my behalf.

I fall on my face today during physio whilst trying to use my arms to push up, unsupported on the plinth. I cry out in pain—or maybe it is more in fear—raw with emotion, worried about what damage I may have caused to my face, still tender from surgery. I sense devastation washing over me as I continually try so hard. Why aren't I healing faster? I just want my arms and legs to work like they used to.

I see the OT twice a week for my hands, the neuropathic pain is crippling, and activities are quite frustrating. The focus is to stimulate movement to prevent my hands becoming claw-like, hence the variety of activities to rebuild dexterity and reduce stiffness. I squeeze bulldog clips today with varying degrees of difficulty. I have a mini splint made for my right hand, which I must wear daily. The purpose of the splint is to prevent the muscles from seizing, which is painful, and also to protect my hand from becoming claw-like. These sessions, although necessary, frustrate me the most due to the constant chronic pain, tingling, and sensitivity in my right arm.

Mum's Diary Note: Multiple activities today at OT session, Kelly does well, but they frustrate her immensely, and I can see she's not a happy person. Hypersensitive as OT rubs her arm.

One month in, I'm commended for being a STAR patient as I work so hard and am dedicated to my physio and rehab activities. The OT exercises for my hands continue to frustrate me, especially those testing my dexterity, with simple tasks like undoing buttons.

Mum's Diary Note: Kelly eating my soup, physio going well with more steps each day, memory test did well, told she's a STAR patient. That's my girl.

There's always something on my mind, today it's the constant worry of my parents catching public transport at night. In my fragile state I explain to Mum how to use Uber, setting up the app and linking it to my credit card. I'll worry about the costs later, I explain, as I almost plead that I need them to be safe. It's another worry for me as they're living in my apartment away from their home in Adelaide.

I Skype my brother, checking in as I gradually uncover the series of events leading to how Mum and Dad found out about my accident. My brother received the call from my emergency contact who found him via LinkedIn. He left work and drove to tell Mum, a schoolteacher, as she was in her classroom and was unreachable.

I FaceTime my niece and nephew, not thinking how heartbreaking it might be for them to see me, neck brace on, and face still swollen as I crook my neck to face my phone, unable to hold it up myself. I'm oblivious as to how this might affect them;

My Hero Skills

my only thought is letting them know I'm okay.

My positivity spills over to the next morning with another small win giving me a boost, as I manage to feed myself breakfast, a few spills, but ... oh well. Next, I take a few steps, albeit while being supported by the physio holding a belt around my waist. It's quite surreal having to relearn a basic function I've been doing most of my life. Feels good to take some steps, have to start somewhere. It's both physically and mentally challenging for me, though in ways I've never experienced before.

One foot in front of the other, intense focus on lifting my foot, controlling my ankle and hip as I bring my leg forward and place it down, all whilst balancing. Next foot, same thing. I think to myself, *how do I cope, how do I do these activities day after day*? I need to dig deep, persevere, as this is my quality of life at stake. I'm at a loss, full of anguish, but know I must keep moving forward, I must acknowledge and celebrate my wins, big or small. Progress over perfection, I will get there. I never thought any differently.

Mum has a day off today; Jacqui kindly takes her out for lunch and a spot of shopping. I'm happy for her, she so deserves this, but I miss her. Thankfully my boyfriend visits and takes me for a spin in my chair outside. Being stuck inside all of the time, I constantly crave the sun on my face. It revitalises me.

Tonight, I call Mum and completely break down. I'm in pain, I'm hurting and I'm extremely emotional.

Crying, I blubber, "WHY ... ?" I'm really struggling, and I can't comprehend the vast array of things happening to me and my body, still feels so foreign. I don't even have the ability to realise the impact my TBI has, frustrated that I'm unable to make sense of things or comprehend the enormity or severity of my injuries.

Everything tumbles around in my head like waves crashing, I'm desperate for them to calm.

Mum's Diary Note: Had a call at 9 pm tonight, Kelly in pain and upset. I listened for about 40 minutes.

I endure life in hospital, and although I feel tremendous sadness, subconsciously, I know my brain is still protecting me with healing being my focus. I adapt as best I can to the hospital environment, doing my best to remain positive, to persevere and to remain tenacious. I'm constantly curious about my surroundings, the daily operations of the hospital, and learning the 'why' around my rehab amongst other activities. My unwavering determination and courage are character building.

Birthday Steps

Nearly six weeks after my accident it's my forty-second birthday. As it nears, the reality is that it will be spent in hospital, in a wheelchair, not knowing what lies ahead of me, or what my future rehabilitation needs look like. Life, as I know it, will be forever different.

It's comforting to know my parents, my bestie Carla, Jacqui, and my boyfriend will all be joining me for birthday celebrations and some cake. I change my dialogue, find a renewed sense of enthusiasm, and work harder than ever. Focused, I take additional steps around the ward, taking every opportunity I can. I decide, with huge amounts of energy and excitement, that for my birthday I will show my loved ones how well I am doing; how hard I'm working and how dedicated I am to being okay. My steadfast resolve and tenacity shines through.

Mum knows my plan, as she has seen me take steps around the ward. She has even bought me cute li'l nonslip slippers for the mornings where I have help to walk to the bathroom. I sit in my chair with them on, clicking my heels together like Dorothy from The Wizard of Oz. It's nice to know that my sense of humour is still intact.

My birthday arrives, and I've coordinated the physios to assist me. I'm pumped, so ready, excited to leave the ward and walk to where my loved ones are waiting.

Nervously, I catch the lift downstairs with the physios. Easing up out of my chair, I stand and begin to walk around the corner, I see everyone in the distance. A physio is close by my side and another one follows with my wheelchair. Butterflies are active in my stomach, a big smile spreads across my face, knowing what I am about to do.

I take slow, concentrated steps forward, I see everyone look up, tears and smiles on their faces as they watch me walk towards them. I know they must be so proud; I am so proud of myself!

I will remember this single moment forever: the feeling of immense achievement.

An emotional and overwhelming moment, especially for Jacqui, who was with me at the time of the accident. We hug, she bends down holding me as I'm now safely in my chair. Carla is her bubbly self—tying a birthday balloon onto the back of my wheelchair. I feel like I have won a race, yet the finish line is still a distance away.

In my mind it is all for them, unselfishly my focus is not on myself today. It's a gift enough: enjoying time with my loved ones, knowing how proud they are of me, and that my hard work is paying off. An immense sense of achievement and love warms my heart.

Mum's Diary Note: Happy Birthday Kelsey!

I struggle to put on a brave face and enjoy the cake, but although it's delicious and Jacqui made my favourite carrot cake, I'm exhausted from walking and all of the excitement. I'm also quite embarrassed at how I look. My crooked smile, tired looking clothes, and what feels like lifeless hair that I struggle to brush. I watch as I see my parents, boyfriend, and closest girlfriends—all smiling for me—with what feels like brave faces.

Birthday Steps

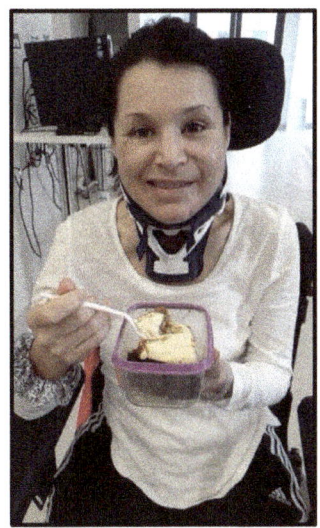
Trying to eat my birthday cake

It is heartbreaking returning to the ward alone after such an amazing high, taking my steps and being with loved ones, to once again being reliant on a buzzer and nurses to help me.

My reality is all too real, and it leaves me grumpy and tired, the neuropathic pain constantly drains me, and the medication provides minimal relief as I retire to bed before 5 pm.

The following day my birthday joy continues with my cycling girls, Ros, Steph, and Margot visiting me. It's so great to see them, I miss our weekly catch-ups and spins out on the open road. Competition as to who can make the best carrot cake. Competitiveness wherever we go, and more laughs. However, I tire and am easily over-stimulated by my visitors; the fatigue due to my brain injury is a constant drain.

My 'work Dad' visits, it's so funny seeing him with my real Dad, and the two of them making jokes about me together feels good. I smile. My boss and a young woman from my team also visit, updating me on what's been happening at work. I feel proud hearing how the young woman I coached is taking the opportunity to shine and to look after the early careers program I built. I'm delighted to hear my legacy is living on and things are well looked after.

Reality Bites

A meeting with all my doctors and specialists: some on Skype and others in the room with Mum, Dad, and me. The topics are: my injuries, the trauma I am undergoing, post-concussion symptoms, my short-term memory loss, and why I am constantly fatigued.

Central cord syndrome, laminectomy—all of the big medical words for the surgery I underwent, and why. The need to relieve pressure on my spinal cord allowing it to swell, and the impact this invasive surgery has on my body. Explains the weakness and numbness in my arms with this main highway of nerves impacted. My face hitting the car's windscreen: a massive knock to my head shaking my brain resulting in my TBI, ongoing fatigue, my inability to think clearly, and the difficulty I have processing information.

My facial injuries, the bone fractures, scars, and the numbness in my lip due to nerve damage. Minor upside, I can have Botox if my lip continues to droop. Always looking at the positive. Mum and I laugh at this, my boyfriend just raises his eyebrows.

There's a lot of discussion around the support I can access for when I leave hospital, but my head isn't there yet, besides I'm thinking maybe I can go home to Adelaide with Mum and Dad. It would be easier to move around their house, as opposed to my unit on the third floor with no lift and three flights of stairs. Vocational and OT support, and I'll need to retest if I want to drive again, I'm advised my license has been suspended. So many different reviews and tests, not to mention what might happen financially as I may be unable to work full-time again. I'm yet to digest the bigger picture of life post-hospital, but for now it's all too overwhelming and incomprehensible.

A conference call with lawyers, my brother joins as he has been managing the legal side of things for me. I need to begin to understand what's happening now and the likely activities moving forward: what things may look like as my life circumstances continually change and my future is impacted.

Sadly, after I eat my scrambled eggs, Mum is stepping up the menu, she leaves, she isn't feeling well. It's been a busy morning.

Having hit my six-week mark, I know the day must be nearing for my neck brace to be removed.

I'm left in my bed in the ward corridor after some scans when a nurse comes up to me smiling, gently she asks me to lift my head forward, and she removes my neck brace. Such an immediate sense of freedom, although my neck feels naked now and quite stiff. Cautiously I move my head a little, yikes, I'm quick to realise half of my head has been shaved. Another thing to tear at my heart.

Then I take the win, and smile as the Tom Petty song 'Free fallin'' enters my head and slowly a whisper escapes my lips as I am wheeled back to my cubicle.

"Yeah, I'm free-ee,
Free-ee fallin."

Gotta love Jerry Maguire!

Night draws near and I must still sleep on my back, how I yearn to roll over, yet I'm relieved the restrictive and uncomfortable brace is off.

The next day I am told I will be moving hospitals, what?! I'm devastated; I knew it was on the cards yet I'm feeling so unprepared for it.

Mum's Diary Note: I'm not going in today I'm not feeling well, think my body has had enough. It is hard to keep going and watching your daughter fighting for her life.

Got a call from Kelly telling us they're moving her to another hospital, POWH. I'm not sure about this as Dr's so good here.

Changing Hospitals

It's little over six weeks post-accident and I'm moved from the comfort of the Royal North Shore Hospital (RNSH), where I had grown to know the nurses and specialists, to the Prince of Wales Hospital (POWH). In the transport vehicle, which is like an ambulance, I feel all alone, worried of what may lie ahead.

I arrive at my new room and I'm flabbergasted to learn that nobody appears to know my medical history. I'm annoyed as I am asked a multitude of questions about my accident and injuries. Halfway through the questioning the nurse realises I'm covered by CTP, so they start completing different forms. Further frustration, my head feels like exploding as I struggle with the incompetence. It's been a big morning and I'm becoming more impatient as I tire.

Feeling frustrated, I ask, "Where are the handover notes? Where do I go to do physio? Who is my OT? Who is my doctor?" The list goes on.

I'm now left to my own devices to shower in a bathroom across the hallway. My excitement of doing things on my own with minimal supervision soon disappears. Really? What if I slip? A single plastic chair, from what looks like an outdoor setting, is placed inside the shower should I need to sit, which I do.

Take me back to RNSH! Crushed, I weep in the shower and return to my room ... alone.

Mum's Diary Note: I'm so sorry Kelly, I'm sick and so weak.

Mum clearly knows I am improving; she's a fighter too, but sadly her body is now giving in, keeping her bedridden for the next ten days. I'm devastated. How will I cope? She is my CONSTANT. I worry what's wrong and if she's okay.

Takes me over a week to figure out how daily physio, OT, and psychologist activities are scheduled. I ask so many questions, desperately trying to understand the operations of my new surroundings: meals, visiting hours, and usage of the common area. I receive bills for my hospital stay, thank goodness for the social workers who explain things and help me reconcile these accounts. Fortunately for me, because the accident isn't my fault, I'm covered under CTP and iCare.

Dad still comes to see me, bless him, but it's not the same. I'm impressed he navigated a bus and the rabbit warren-like hospital to find my room. Aww thanks, Pa.

Jacqui brings dinner for us, how nice is this. My favourite too, salmon, soft and easy for me to eat. We sit and catch up, her smiley, happy personality is infectious. I'm so grateful and I'm feeling blessed by her kindness. Dessert too, delicious. Feeling all the feels today.

It's time for the pins to be removed from my jaw, and a patient transfer vehicle is arranged to take me back to RNSH for my appointment. Anxious. I'm not filled with confidence that I will make it on time as I've been advised the transport vehicles aren't reliable. I shake my head when I'm told they can't be booked for a specific time. I don't want to miss my surgery, it's more anxiety

Changing Hospitals

and frustration on top of the fact I'm scared about being anaesthetised again. My body, which is still weak, has been through so much already.

I make it on time and soon find myself making jokes with the surgeon to hide my nerves. I see the bright lights overhead as I'm wheeled into the operating theatre, and then close my eyes and nod off, the anaesthetic kicks in quickly.

Thankfully, when I wake I feel a bit groggy, but okay. Soon afterwards I have a drink and a few mouthfuls of sandwich before being taken back to POW.

Good news, Mum doesn't have Covid-19, however, she's still feeling unwell. We chat every day, but it's not the same. Dad visits and enjoys all the goodies my visitors bring. Karyn, my emergency contact, visits and holds me tightly, pleasantly surprised at how mobile I am and how well I look. She talks me through how she tracked down my brother, her late pet rabbit sharing the same name. It's good to laugh.

I'm relocated to another room, as I am walking around more now and with increased stability.

I had postponed having my catheter taken out, not knowing how I might react to 'going under' to remove the screws from my jaw, but I am ready now. The catheter has become uncomfortable because I'm walking around more and more, not to mention that my body is rejecting it. I even woke up with a wet bed, super embarrassing. OMG, I'm not five!

I'm advised I need to wait—wait for what?! Urology is only available once a week. Now who's cranky, hey!

I am aware there is another option—education is gold, my friends—and I ask about 'trial of void'. I could see the doctor hesitate, insisting I wait for urology. I'm sure there is steam coming out of my ears, as I'm fuming.

Now I'm deflated, thinking *'Why do I need to drive my own rehab?'* I desperately want my catheter out, it's so uncomfortable and it's restrictive during physio. Also, I want to do hydrotherapy, as Covid-19 restrictions have eased the hospital is opening the pool. I'm working so hard and making progress with my mobility, and being weightless in the water would be beneficial for my recovery, and it would feel *so* nice.

I have some tests, excited as time nears for my catheter to be removed. Sadly I have a 'bug', so it remains in, and I must take antibiotics. I miss out on hydrotherapy, I'm gutted, I feel so miserable. I'm frustrated when it happens again the following week, and I take another set of antibiotics. I ask the doctor, "How many bugs are there?" Impatiently, I boldly ask about trial of void again and I leave smiling when it's arranged for later that afternoon.

Finally, I do the trial of void tests and I pass. Success. My catheter is taken out after eight weeks of discomfort, and who knows what damage to my system, but it's out. I'm delighted that I listened to my body and had the courage to speak up. I'm so relieved.

Next morning I wake up and instantly check my sheets, they're dry—winning! I still visited urology a few days later, pleased to learn all was okay.

Mum's Diary Note: On the bus to see Kelsey, it's been 11 days, I can't wait to hug her.

It's so good to see Mum, we hug one another, tears streaming down our faces.

Mum's Back!! And I'm On The Move Again

I slowly begin to improve, and I am again asked to move rooms. I pack after breakfast, and when I return after physio I discover that my belongings have been relocated to a room further from the front desk. Checking my old room, I'm annoyed to find the whiteboard cleared of my notes. It's how I keep track of what's happening, questions I've asked the doctor, or things I'm waiting an answer on. My short-term memory isn't what it used to be, and with so many things happening it's how I keep a sense of control. I also have a weekly timetable on the whiteboard with my various therapies, which is helpful when planning time for my visitors.

Pleased I have my own room with a shower—providing me with some privacy—I try to write down what I remember, trusting things will come to me over the next few days. I shake my head at the sight of renovations taking place on the far wall, it looks like a sink has been removed. I'm interrupted early next morning as the renovations continue, alarmed but not really surprised. Who does that? It's a hospital, people! The wall is fixed over the next few days, followed by painting which leaves a lingering smell. Clearly, I am unimpressed by it all.

Again, I receive incorrect medication, albeit in a different hospital, but I'm not impressed. Thankfully I'm 'present' when it comes to my wellbeing, especially where medication is concerned. I'm dumbfounded that this has happened again. Inconsistent support from nurses appalls me; I appreciate it's a taxing job, but we are sick people so give us a smile and some empathy. Some nurses just have this energy, which I love, and a sense of humour which helps you get through difficult days and forget about your pain, just for a moment. Others are disappointing, but I don't know everyone's circumstances, so I value the nurses who smile, and I smile back at them.

Food remains tasteless, it doesn't appear nourishing, and I wonder how patients are meant to heal. Thankfully Mum continues to bring me nutritious food. Feels like I've been here forever and the better I get the more impatient and intolerant I become.

My room is constantly cold, exacerbating the neuropathic pain in my right arm. At nights I begin to feel so alone, and as I slowly improve the frequency of visitors decreases. Sadness envelopes me as Mum and Dad come and leave each day. I move around the hospital without my chair, even making myself a cup of tea, just the way I like it. Mum has bought me my own milk which is kept in the fridge with my name on it. Gee it's good, the little, simple pleasures. I often feel guilty walking around the ward, as others aren't as mobile. My thoughts go to my cosy, warm home, I don't want to be here, but the reality is I'm not yet capable of looking after myself.

I struggle constantly with fatigue as I continue to push myself in two sessions of physio every day, have OT three times a week, attend a session with the psychiatrist, juggle visitors, and deal with the discomfort of pain in the left side of my chest, neuropathic pain, and limited movement in my right arm. I have a lot going on. I know I'm in denial about the enormity of my injuries as I continue pushing through my daily activities. Yet I've already enquired about reducing my medication, as I'm not a fan of taking drugs.

I experience a rollercoaster of emotions and moods: often feeling useless, lost, and not myself. I'm still reliant on nurses to help me do simple daily tasks, such as putting my hair up, as I'm not capable of lifting my arms above my head. I do eventually come up with the bright idea to lay across the single bed and dangle my head backwards so I can put my hair up myself. It's easier not pushing my arms against gravity. I'm cautious though, as leaning backwards makes me dizzy and lightheaded.

Back in my wheelchair, I'm allowed to head outside; fortunately the hospital is in Randwick, Sydney, with shops and pubs nearby and accessible. Mum brings in a few more clothes for me as we are heading out to lunch.

Real food, fresh flavours burst in my mouth. Such a delicious sensation after all the tasteless food I have been eating. It's nice to enjoy being out with Mum and Dad, and to treat them after everything they have been doing for me. My bestie's mum and partner join us too, and it feels so civilised ... and almost normal. I fidget constantly and struggle to relax although I'm out of my chair and seated inside the pub. The noisy environment doesn't help as I struggle to engage in conversation, the additional effort required to focus and concentrate is a side effect of my brain injury.

The following day, I'm pleased that Mum and Dad take the day off, friends take Mum to the shops and for lunch—they deserve a break. I head out to dinner with Jacqui, I'm so excited, little Miss Social. Lol!

We head to a restaurant close to the hospital and enjoy a lovely dinner and catch up just like old times, as if nothing has happened. However, I tire quickly and as we go to head back to the hospital we gasp with surprise as it's pouring outside. Neither of us has an umbrella and, confined to my wheelchair, I clearly can't run back. Fortunately, Jacqui remains calm and quickly comes up with the clever idea of heading across the road to the local chemist and buys two waterproof ponchos. Laughing, we head back to the hospital in our ponchos only getting mildly wet from the rain.

Hydrotherapy time! Finally, three weeks and a couple of rounds of antibiotics later. Let's do this. Mum has brought in my bathers; I laugh, realising how hairy my legs are. Fortunately my care factor isn't high, it's the least of my worries. As I walk down the ramp and enter the pool I think of how nice and easy being weightless in the water, and the smooth motion of swirling my arms around, will be. Caution quickly kicks in after I nearly slip down the ramp. Not many patients are allowed in the pool, so it is a privilege I don't want to lose.

Staying in the shallow end I swirl my arms around, bringing my legs up and ... start sinking. Yep, remaining afloat is harder than I had anticipated. I continue trying though, and the physio shows me different activities using my whole body, and floating aids keep it challenging, interesting, and fun. Nice to have the variety after so many weeks in the gym. As a result of my spinal cord injury, my arms are the weakest link. The highway of messaging down my spine is damaged, and the side streets that lead to my

Mum's Back!! And I'm On The Move Again

arms are struggling to receive their operational messages. This is how it is described to me. Luckily I am stubborn and persistent, ha! ha! I am determined and, having achieved some improvement, I know doing the physio works. I want my arms to work properly, but more than that deep down I just want to be okay and that is what's driving me.

I get out of the pool, quickly towel dry myself, and put on my checked dressing gown, the perfect ensemble post-swim to keep me warm. I walk back onto the ward giggling at my fashion sense, of course smiling at a few people I pass before entering my room for a hot shower. It was all too hard to take my stuff and shower at the pool. Besides, it's how we respond, cope, and continue to grow when things happen to us, and I'm just doing the best I can.

I love having visitors, and it's even nicer when it's 'too easy' for them to pick up my parents. I'm so grateful for my amazing friends and work colleagues whose generosity means so much. More homemade biscuits are a welcome treat. The effort made to visit, to spend time catching up, and having a laugh is the best medicine for me. As they say, 'kindness is free'.

Outside of these visits my therapy continues incorporating skills that not only help my hands, but include movements required in preparation for my return to everyday life outside of hospital. Cooking is a passion of mine and is a welcome activity to assist with me with rebuilding these skills, macrame not so much. The hospital has a fully equipped kitchen onsite, so I give Mum a list of ingredients to buy at the local grocery store. I'm excited to be allowed to use the kitchen to cook as part of my OT sessions, and it provides me with a sense of achievement, especially as it doubles as dinner for Mum and Dad.

Breaking Up With My Wheelchair

I'm excited for this morning's physio session as I finally get to walk outside. I'm up, shower on my own, eat breakfast, get dressed, and down the hall I head.

Progressing from strength to strength I feel good, fortunately I had a decent level of fitness prior to my accident (cycling one hundred kilometres on a weekend, walking seven kilometres into the city for work, and regular swimming and Pilates sessions … the list goes on) and I apply myself continually in my daily physio sessions. I realise I've already progressed from being able to walk around the ward to, today, heading outside. I'll be accompanied for my safety, and to see how I go navigating footpaths and kerbs, and crossing the road. I'm excited though as this is significant in me being on my way to regaining my independence. Freedom is all I can think about walking through the exit doors of the hospital and heading outside. Feeling the sunshine on my face I smile as I walk and chat with the physios, careful to watch where I'm going, consciously lifting and lowering my feet.

A wave of happiness soon washes over me as I'm told I have passed my walking assessment outdoors unassisted. I'm on my way, I quietly think, just keep moving forwards. Wahoo, go me!

I sigh with relief, momentarily proud of myself, another feather in my cap. A booster showing me the *Art of the Possible* …

Breaking Up With My Wheelchair

The hard things never get easier, we just get stronger.

Unbelievable. After an amazing morning out I'm told I need to move rooms again. Frustrated, I pack my belongings and decide to leave my wheelchair behind; I don't need it anymore. I have rebuilt enough strength, retrained my brain, and as a result I am well on my way to walking safely unassisted.

Walking feels normal, yet not quite natural: my steps don't flow, but hey, I'm walking. Every now and then my body surprises me, especially as I'm not a particularly patient person and I've been at this learning to walk again thing for nearly two months. This was one race I couldn't rush.

A nurse tries to wheel the chair into my new room, but I announce that I don't need it anymore, we are done, we have broken up! I chuckle, not sure Mum is happy with my abruptness, but hey, this relationship was over. My determination to keep moving forwards and live my best life is well underway.

Working hard at physio, it's comforting to see noticeable results, and this is the liberating moment I break up with my wheelchair, there is no going back for me, we are done!

Every week something seems to happen to help keep my spirits raised and to remind me just how lucky I am. Such as appreciating a win—big or small—a visitor, a message or a phone call, a positive therapy session, good test results, or a nice night nurse to name a few. After living in Sydney for over twenty years, it is nice for my parents to see firsthand the supportive friendships and community I have built around me.

My workplace has been unreal, sending meals to Mum and Dad, helping my brother with legal dealings, whilst making sure I access any benefits I'm entitled to so I continue to be paid. Today

Breaking Up With My Wheelchair

Mum tells me I need to be available at 1 pm to join a Zoom call from work. Odd, but I don't think too much about it.

I sit with Mum in my room and dial into the call where I receive a personalised message from my CEO, my HR Director, and messages of encouragement and well wishes from our Pro Cycling team. I'm speechless, Wow! I just happen to work for a global company that coincidently sponsors a Pro Cycling Team, that I'd met earlier in the year at the Tour Down Under (TDU) cycling event in Adelaide.

This whole sequence of events is quite surreal and takes me by surprise. I sit not moving, quiet, and in disbelief. Mum has tears in her eyes, sharing my progress. The icing on the cake is when, in closing, they share that $5000 has been donated to the Amy Gillett Foundation on my behalf. The Amy Gillett Foundation is Australia's leading cycling safety organisation, driven by a core mission to reduce the death and injury of cyclists. I'm sure my jaw would've dropped if it could have. What a buzz, such a thoughtful gesture for one of our executives to organise. It's something I will never forget, such generosity and kindness, touching and so meaningful.

This day continues to get better with more homemade goodies: a salmon risotto from fellow cycling friend, Tash; plus she baked Carol's famous choc chip cookies. Carol is another friend who lives interstate and is unable to visit. Romy has made one of her famous soft and spongy cinnamon cakes, and some cashew butter—get out! All very delicious, and perfect timing as I need the sustenance now as I walk more and more.

Clocking up two kilometres outside today with the physio, and I'm beaming with happiness. I must say I am enjoying walking to the kitchen and making myself a cup of tea, just the way I like it, mmm. Once again, the small things I used to take for granted are now a big deal that signifies improvement. How I missed my cup of tea, a simple pleasure.

I'm constantly aware of what my parents are giving up to be here with me, and I want to do something nice with them. Now I can walk a bit more, I seek approval and organise a day out. We catch a cab to the local shopping centre. It's so nice to be in a different environment and to feel a little bit normal walking around. We enjoy a lovely lunch before I realise I've pushed myself too hard, sadly my body isn't able to cope with all the activity and we return to the hospital.

Mum's Diary Note: Kelly very emotional today, snapping at us, so leave without giving her a hug, breaks my heart, this is so tough on me too.

I'm devastated that Mum leaves without giving me a hug, and I sob, reflecting on the rollercoaster of the past weeks that is my life. From having control of my body, my thoughts, and my feelings as an able-bodied forty-something adult to finding myself in hospital trying to comprehend the impact and enormity of my accident, the injuries I'm left with, and not knowing what's next for me, struggling to adjust and to make sense of things, no doubt due to my TBI. And the weird world of the pandemic and associated restrictions isn't helping, as I struggle to grasp conceptually what is happening. Pull your head in Kel, Mum is doing the best she can. I call and apologise.

The following day is better, less tiring, we stay local and Mum and I have manicures whilst Dad enjoys a coffee. Funny how something so small once again signifies my improvement and helps me to feel, albeit slowly, some sense of normality.

Research completed, enquiries made, I'm now transitioning into my GSD mode—Get Sh*t Done! Yay for my Hero Skills. Post injury that's what I'm calling them. I feel some sense of steering my rehab, of taking control, and although it's a small step it feels good. And upon reflection it is actually quite significant in me driving my own healing.

I've arranged to see a local orthodontist to enquire what can be done with my now misaligned teeth. Because my jaw has been broken, my upper and lower teeth don't connect properly on one side of my mouth. This misaligned 'bite' makes it extremely difficult to chew, even as my face continues to settle. I'm sent for x-rays, and I return only to be told no work can be undertaken for twelve months as my face needs further time to heal, post major surgery. So, my crooked smile remains, as does my soft food diet. Urgh, I try to be positive, thinking I'm lucky to have my own teeth, I guess.

On the upside, the orthodontist has his oral maxillo-facial surgeon on site, who examines my face and recommends I use Dermatix gel to help fade the scar near my right eye. We find it at the local Chemist Warehouse on our way back to the hospital. Dad has great pleasure massaging my scar hard with the gel, to break it down. Another big day of walking leaves me exhausted.

The next thing on my mind is Mum's birthday, and once again feelings of guilt arise as she is away from her friends. I sigh as I wonder how I can make it special. Centennial Park is nearby and thankfully it's a nice place for lunch, so I ring and secure a booking. This makes me happy. 😊

Mum is delighted I've made plans for lunch; I can see it in her eyes. It's such an effort for me though to get dressed, with my hands stiff and numb. I fumble trying to grip my jeans to do up my zipper and button, and the simple act of putting in earrings is frustrating to manage. Looking at my face in the mirror as I apply mascara leaves me sad. It's me, but it's not me looking back, which is confronting. I do my best to shrug it off telling myself it's Mum's day. I take a deep breath, apply some gloss and am ready to go, exhausted before we've even left.

Mum's Diary Note: We arrive for lunch and Kelly is all dressed, she looks so pretty, hair done, mascara on. She's come a long way; we are all so lucky. Lovely birthday lunch. Thanks Kelsey xx

Mum's smile makes my morning struggles worthwhile. Thankfully lunch is delicious. It's strange, yet nice, to be away from ho-hum days of therapy in the hospital. I'm pleased I make it a nice day for Mum. Silently giving myself a high-five as I organise with the staff a candle in a friand for Mum. 'Happy Birthday' my angel, my saviour.

Goal Posts Shift— Time To Pivot

It's time. I've been in hospital now for over two months, but it feels so much longer. Social workers share with me the approach the hospital takes when organising exit activities and what needs to happen.

I have already spoken briefly to Mum about returning home to Adelaide with her and Dad, logically this makes sense. Their house is big enough, all on the one level, and I'd have their support. Besides, I live alone on the third floor of an apartment block only accessible by stairs, how would I cope? Mum is happy with this decision.

Meeting with all my therapists and social workers, we discuss my progress and what my transition back out into the real world will look like, inclusive of any support I would receive. Fortunately, because the accident was not my fault, I am entitled to carers, amongst other support services; it's covered as a part of the driver's CTP. It's a huge relief having not incurred any medical bills to date, passing any hospital bills which come through to the social workers to look after.

The social workers advocate for me in these group meetings, articulating what I can't. I feel they have my best interests at heart and I'm so grateful for them.

Breaking Up With My Wheelchair

Mum's Diary Note: Bad news, may not be able to take Kelly home due to Covid restrictions.

I'm devastated when I'm notified that I'm denied a medical exemption from isolating for two weeks in Adelaide, and additionally I'm not permitted to enter hospital so I can continue my intensive physio amongst other therapies. Now what, people?! Unbelievable. Words escape me, steam is likely billowing out of my ears once again as I try to process this absurd and unfair message.

Returning to my apartment, living and coping on my own is now my only option. Time to pivot!

The physiotherapist shares the importance of relearning to not only climb, but descend, stairs safely. Easy enough, right? Pffft!

GAME ON!

It's the small movements now that have the biggest impact; the focus is on controlling my ankle and foot movements, and this requires extreme concentration which, as an adult, would usually come naturally. Now I must relearn to consciously navigate the stairwell daily, just add it to my list of things to concentrate on, which exhausts me mentally and physically. Who would've thought?

Time alone at night gives me the opportunity to read through documents from the social workers, lawyers, and various insurance companies as I try to piece together what is happening and what I might be entitled to moving forward. My main driver is this constant feeling of being a burden on my family and, although not directly my fault, I feel responsible. The iCare organisation appears to be quite supportive, and I feel some form of win when I have the cost of my parents' flights refunded.

Goal Posts Shift—Time To Pivot

There's so much more to understand and figure out, but this leaves me feeling positive and as though I am gaining some form of understanding of the system.

I'm ignorant to the facts, at this point anyway, about my financial situation, and that my ability to return to work full-time in the future is highly unlikely. This is due to my TBI, management of chronic pain, fatigue, and the ongoing need for physio and specialist appointments. Unbeknown to me my healing will be constant, a lifelong journey of management. My poor body has, is, and will continue to go through so much.

All systems go, I will be returning to my apartment in a matter of weeks. I freeze, not sure how I feel about this, having been reliant on others for so long. I'm aware how much of a struggle returning to my apartment alone will be: navigating three flights of stairs, and not to mention carrying groceries, and the daily tasks of cooking and washing. A few steps forward and even more backward. I sigh, knowing it needs to happen, and if not now … when? I push on and focus on what needs to be done, looking at my end goal: *wanting to leave hospital.*

So I may return to my unit and regain my independence a home visit is organised with my OT. This is to review which adaptations will be required so I can live safely in my home. I become nervous when I verbalise this visit to Mum, it's real, it's happening. Feels daunting, unsure what my place will look like with Mum's and Dad's belongings there and, no doubt, things moved around. I try and voice this cyclone of thoughts to my psychologist, however it's difficult to unpack, to express myself with so many feelings tumbling around in my head. I'm unable to think clearly and process the bigger picture of what the visit represents.

Mum's Diary Note: Clean up time as Kelly is visiting her place

Breaking Up With My Wheelchair

Friday, how exciting. 😊

My thoughts go to Mum and Dad: when I return home where will they go?

I know Mum isn't ready to leave me yet, and if I'm honest with myself I want her to stay, I need her. We have such a special bond; we always have had.

The OT and I arrive at my unit, I don't even know what we talked about in the car, it's like I'm in a state of numbness, apprehensive about the visit. We buzz the intercom; Mum lets us in. The single fact is it's familiar, it's my home, and climbing the stairs is symbolic of the next stage of Kelly-Anne, post this life-changing event. Breathing deeply, I take the stairs one by one, pacing myself, conscious of my feet and ankles, holding onto the rail. I'm doing it!

I can sense Mum watching me even before I round the corner of the last flight. I look up and see her standing, holding the door open and watching me. Tears glistening in her blue eyes, an emotional time for the both of us, having been so close these last three months on this rollercoaster together. Final few steps, I make it and wrap my arms around her frail body, hugging her oh-so gently. No words, just tears streaming down our faces.

Mum's Diary Note: Very emotional, yet so proud watching her walk up the stairs!

It's odd seeing my parents and their belongings spread out in my tiny apartment. Dad in the spare room on a blow-up mattress, my old bike and indoor trainer all packed up. Was I more upset about the trainer or Dad's sleeping arrangements I wonder briefly. At least they have the comfort of my place, some familiarity as opposed to being somewhere foreign. They are

Goal Posts Shift—Time To Pivot

both in good spirits having found everything they need, including the all-important bottle shop and Woolworths, within one hundred metres from my front door. Phew. Oh, and whatever booze I had is now gone. Not high on my list of things to worry about, but it made Dad happy. Parents, hey!

Thankfully, only a few modifications will be required to accommodate my injuries: non-slip bathmats, a stool in the shower to sit on, some kitchen utensils to support my limited hand movement. Plus, the inclusion of care and support workers to assist with my grocery shopping and cleaning.

That night back at the hospital I reflect on my day with mixed excitement and apprehension around returning to my place. How do I regain my independence? A sense of worry, fear, and distress overcomes me. There's so many emotions, and so much to deal with.

Mum's Diary Note: OT is happy with the unit. Sad to see Kelsey go. ☹

Trial Sleep-Overs

Luckily, I'm constantly curious, and I overhear another patient discussing their overnight stay on the weekend with a nurse. Really? Why wasn't this offered to me? Everything just frustrates me here. I listen for a bit longer trying to understand more about these overnight stays. I soon enquire and am told, yes, it is an option for me. My heart fills with joy. I call my boyfriend immediately, excited to share this news and set to work on organising my overnight stay.

Surprise, surprise, there's more frustration with the process being unclear, I need multiple therapists to sign off on my overnight stay. All that excitement has gone as I'm devastated, thanks to *more* miscommunication. The draining rollercoaster of life in the spinal cord ward has left me an emotional wreck. I seek out my therapists individually, request sign off, and submit my forms. I await impatiently for my approval. I don't need to write a reminder on my whiteboard to follow this up. I want it so badly; I know I'll remember it.

I focus on something more positive to shift my mood, and I'm soon chuffed with myself having arranged for Mum and me to see my fabulous hairdresser. As long as I sign in and out, I can come and go as I please during the daytime, so I make the most of this freedom. My hair definitely needs some TLC and a cut will help me begin to *feel* normal, albeit that I'm far from it, but it's definitely a start. So much fun to share this with Mum and for her to have a haircut by a "Sydney Hairdresser", she is so delighted.

John, my Scissor Queen, has been my hairdresser for nearly fifteen years, and he is delighted to meet Mum.

Any smile I put on my Mum's face, after everything she is doing for me, both energises me and makes me happy.

Mum's Diary Note: Mum and Daughter haircuts. So fun and great to see her smile and laugh a lot.

My boyfriend picks us up afterwards, and we all enjoy dinner at the local pub before taking my parents home, and sadly dropping me back to the hospital. Such a sense of sadness and loneliness as I walk the stale halls back to my room. These activities help me to begin to transition away from the comforts and familiarity of the hospital. Yet they also pain me with feelings of conflict: I'm scared at the thought of leaving the comfort of the hospital, yet I desperately want to return to the real world and my life. Tired, sad, and alone in my room I try not to overthink things, I play some newfound sleepy music to calm my mind and my nervous system and help me drift off to sleep.

Reflection: Unbeknown to me at this point, my life will be constantly filled with challenges and change as I forge a new normal, as I try my hardest to rebuild and heal. I don't know it yet, but three years on I will realise the *essence of me will always be within and will live on.*

It's group meeting time again, and discussions continue around my needs for my exit and transition home. A lot of actions still need to happen as I voice what I'd like much more clearly now, with support from the social workers. My departure date is confirmed. The countdown is on: three weeks until I'm outta here, yeh, bring it!

Beaming, I've a renewed sense of energy, plus the approval for

Trial Sleep-Overs

my overnight stay with my boyfriend comes through, followed by a weekend stay at my place with Mum and Dad. Feeling hopeful I smile, acknowledging my progress, quietly knowing I'll be okay, forever a fighter.

Small overnight bag packed, and I head to my boyfriend's apartment; I tackle more stairs. Somewhere so familiar, yet it's feeling so foreign. Awkward and fidgety, I try and relax in a space I'm usually comfortable in. Delicious salmon dinner, one of my favourites, a bit of TV, I take my medication and crawl into bed. No nurses, no blood pressure taken, no cold hospital room or noises from the ward, but I still feel quite restless. What feels like an awkward cuddle, I lie on my back staring at the ceiling before I eventually doze off.

The next few days are filled with therapy, amongst other appointments, as things are all GO for my return home. Poor Mum and Dad have a timetable to juggle their visits around, and I don't see much of them. I organise a lovely Italian dinner at a restaurant close by as a treat for all of us. Trying not to think of what lies ahead, the reality of returning home is all too real and approaching fast.

I have been madly searching for Airbnb stays, amongst other accommodation, locally for Mum and Dad. I've reassured Mum I will look after it, it's important I sort something, yet nothing seems right nor within my budget. I am also keen to reduce my medication and get rid of some of this brain fog I am experiencing on a daily basis, so I may better manage the multitude of activities taking place. I chase the various doctors, but more proactivity on my behalf is proving exhausting. Surprisingly this is an easy and quick win with the doctors comfortable with me reducing my medication. I feel way more comfortable to tackle this change whilst in the safe confines of the hospital.

Breaking Up With My Wheelchair

As I lay awake it dawns on me that my work has several serviced apartments that aren't being used, due to the Covid-19 pandemic. Could I? Can I ask? I think to myself. Absolutely, they have been so great to me, and many times they have told me to reach out if they can help in any way. A serviced apartment would be so convenient, accessible by bus from the city to my place. I draw up enough courage and call my HR Director, nervously I ask her, and I remain optimistic when she happily advises she will ask the CEO and get back to me asap.

I receive a 'yes' within a few hours.

Grinning from ear to ear, I proudly share with Mum and Dad that I have sorted their accommodation, no need to worry. A two-bedroom, two-bathroom, fully self-contained apartment compliments of my work within the Swissotel in the city. Yeh, GO Me! I think I probably gave myself a cheeky high-five. Even as I verbalised this to my parents it didn't seem real.

I'm delighted that being brave and asking for help has paid off, an amazing outcome securing a place for my parents close by that they will be comfortable in. A huge relief for me and, no doubt, for them too.

A visit back to RNSH for some x-rays—they're happy with my spine, which is wonderful news.

The weekend is here, time to head home with Mum and Dad, it's going to be a cosy one sharing my place for the weekend. Having now had a night away from the hospital, now I just want out of here. I juggle all of the uneasy feelings of returning to my space, knowing I'll be safe with Mum there. So nice to be in the comfort and warmth of my own home and bed. I sleep well. Mum insists she'll be fine sleeping on the couch.

Trial Sleep-Overs

The next day, Mum and I have lunch with two of my work colleagues, senior women, one of whom has kids and I sense that she admires Mum and her strength. Lovely, intelligent, and caring ladies who are happy to see I'm doing well.

I try to act normally, engage in conversation, and ignore my pain, however, it's a struggle. On the positive side it is nice to share this lunch with Mum, I am extremely proud of her along with all of the strong women in my life.

I'm fortunate I was raised so well, quality values instilled in me that saw me thrive when I moved from Adelaide to Sydney at just twenty-two years of age.

Mum's Diary Note: Great to sit and watch TV and have a lazy night at home with Kelsey. She slept well, no drugs. 😊

Next morning, I take Mum and Dad on the bus into the city so they will know how to get to their new accommodation. We don't go inside as it will be another few days before we are given the keys.

Feels quite odd returning to the hospital later that afternoon, my things are in the room, yet it feels so cold and unwelcoming. I crawl into the stiff single bed, and the familiar noises of the ward return. I call and say goodnight to Mum, thanking her for a nice weekend and for all of her help. The night nurse brings my medication, and takes my blood pressure, activities I won't miss. Headphones and sleepy music on, I drift off to sleep.

Mum's Diary Note: So quiet without Kelly here.

The countdown is on, a few more days until I return home, I can hardly believe it. I'm ready now, apprehensive, but ready. Sometimes we must "feel the fear and do it anyway", shift our thoughts and move *through* the anxiety.

A final meeting with all my therapists confirms that they've actively engaged with, and provided handover notes to, my new therapists external to the hospital. I'm thankful to hear some are local, especially my Exercise Physiologist (EP) and Occupational Therapist (OT), both of whom who I will see weekly. So much planning and co-ordination of logistics for my departure.

The meetings continue, with an outplacement nurse educating me on what to be aware of as my body will continue to change and heal. Wow, so much, I'm thankful there are notes, and I'll read them again later as I'm sure I don't take everything in. More x-rays and check-ups with the good news that all is going well. Mum and Dad come and go as I begin sending my belongings home with them. Busy few days.

I meet my iCare manager, who seems quite nice. She shares with me which rehab activities are funded, how anything 'reasonable and necessary' is also taken care of, what her role is, and how we will work together once I'm released. The system is all new to me, hence a lot of questions to ask and education to acquire so I can access the best care. I get the sense there is a lot to sort through, but my focus is on going home so I park my thoughts, aiming to deal with things as they arise.

Finally, everything is signed off, tomorrow I am being released. I fill out some forms in preparation for my departure. I thank my therapists as I complete my final sessions in the hospital wondering, *is this really happening?* I say goodbye to a few more people and leave a small gift and card for the social workers who helped me immensely, always so patient, supportive and kind.

Feels strange walking the ward knowing I'm leaving; it's so familiar, having been my home for what feels like forever.

Moving day for Mum and Dad goes well, they're happy with the

Trial Sleep-Overs

apartment, which is a relief. I'm excited I'll be seeing them tomorrow when I return home. Things are coming together.

Mum's Diary Note: Moving day for Kevin and I. Wow, the apartment is Swish!

PART TWO: Home

Home Time— Three Months And One Day

Today I head home, finally it's here. Had a restless night, but I'm not worried as my focus is to look and move forwards, and this day is HUGELY significant. I feel immensely proud of myself, excited as I get ready and attend to final sign offs, collect my medications, and silently walk my final length of the Spinal Cord Ward at POWH.

Thanks, see ya!

I feel such sadness for those remaining in the ward, I wish them well, and pray they find strength and believe in themselves.

Thirteen weeks, three months and one day, or ninety-two days—whatever way you look at it it's a *long* time, feels longer accounting for everything that's happened to me, and it's still baffling for me to get my head around it all.

I survived being hit by a car, two major life saving spinal surgeries, a broken jaw, and I learnt to walk again ... phenomenal, go me and my Hero Skills.

My boyfriend is waiting, the biggest hug, he loads the car and we head home. A quite surreal feeling, even more so as I walk up *my* stairs and enter *my* place. 'Home, sweet home,' I smile.

Mum and Dad are here to welcome me, which is comforting. I unpack as Mum and I reorganise my place to the way I like it. Luckily, I live close to the shops so a little walk grabbing a few groceries, and slowly I feel a bit more settled. I push down all the overwhelming thoughts of how the coming days might unfold, and the fact that I need to think about what I want to eat, cook for myself … blah, blah, blah. Boring. I try not over think it.

First night on my own I'm simply happy enjoying the peace, and being in the comfort and warmth of my own bed. Pleased I'd had a few trial nights away from the hospital to ease into being on my own, at peace I nod off.

Nice to wake up naturally, light streaming through my window, seeing the trees, no nurses needing to take my blood pressure, no hospital noises. Being undisturbed and not having to be anywhere at any particular time is bliss. Not to mention I have slept like a log.

Carla is visiting in a few hours, I take my time getting ready, I'm light-hearted and at ease surrounded by my things at home. It's very quiet and a little lonely, but that's okay.

Delighted to see her, a big squeeze, no you won't break me, we laugh. She's a breath of fresh air, her ongoing support, kindness and friendship is unwavering. #grateful

I later head to see Mum and Dad's new digs, excited as Mum is cooking her famous crumbed chicken; my boyfriend and his daughter are joining us, and I will sleep over. Comforting to see them settled in a nice, homely space and enjoying dinner with everyone. Fun night.

Home Time—Three Months And One Day

The next day it feels great to socialise with more friends, reconnect and enjoy a nice lunch, plus share it with Mum. It's pleasing to see her smile after everything she's sacrificed for me. We always had a pretty special bond, but this is next level. I consider myself to be a very lucky daughter.

Mum's Diary Note: Beautiful lunch with the girls, Great to see Kelly laughing and having fun. 😊

The next few weeks involve a lot of juggling my mess of a life post-hospital. Support services and therapists that were meant to be organised weren't, and I'm once again left to project manage things and take action so I can get on with my life. Thankfully, Mum and Dad are still around, and although it's helpful they can begin to see I'm coping okay. I'm not sure how sometimes, but that's the beauty of my support network.

I learn to work through hiccups, albeit frustratingly, and get on with living, doing the best I can. Acknowledging, and very much aware, that it's okay to get upset, to be disappointed, and to be frustrated, but not to dwell in what can be a horrible, negative space. Continually looking and moving forwards, smiling, and talking to friends is what helps me through. Healing takes time and I need to be comfortable with being uncomfortable within a space of uncertainty. I don't like it, nor am I good at it, but I accept it and do my best.

Conscious of feedback from a therapist I had seen years before, I know I will feel better if I actively make plans to fill my days. Life is here to live, so my mood shifts, my pain seems that little bit lessened, I'm not focusing on my crooked smile, my droopy cheek or the scar near my eye.

Jacqui and her husband join us for dinner, and once again Mum cooks a delicious meal. It's wonderful to see her, to catch up and share that I'm doing okay out of hospital. I enjoy a glass of champagne, the bubbles swirling around my mouth; a taste and delight I have missed. Only one glass for me, as alcohol isn't advised in the early stages of recovering from a TBI.

A pleasant evening, however, I tire early and feel a bit woozy after the bubbles. With my brave face on I wish the guests a goodnight, and soon after they leave I go to bed.

My whole world has been turned upside-down, and it's not easy forming a new normal as I'm definitely in no position to return to my old life, unsure if I ever will be. Every day brings a new challenge, and I am well aware the countdown is on until Mum and Dad return to Adelaide and I must learn to cope on my own.

Building My New-Normal Life

Finally, my rehab specialists and other support services seem to be in place. I've organised transport to get to appointments, okay I have multiple cab charges, but hey, that's better than public transport. My request for physio two to three times a week has been approved so I'm super happy with myself, knowing that physio is the key to me getting stronger. Spending over three months in hospital has left me thin, weak, and with little muscle. A new general practitioner (GP) that's closer to home is sorted and, I'm building my understanding of what I have access to from iCare: how to be reimbursed for things I've paid for that are reasonable and necessary for my recovery.

A positive outcome from meeting with multiple therapists is that I am constantly learning about my injuries, my recovery, and what is available to me. Today's win is that I am allowed to reapply for my driver's licence ... actually I never realised I'd lost it. In my instance it's only suspended, and I must retest so it may be reactivated.

Bring it!

In the meantime I'm busy with legalities, and sessions for physiotherapy, exercise physiology, occupational therapy, trauma psychology, and Skin LED light therapy, plus appointments with the neurologist, dentist, and iCare support worker, as well as driving lessons, the list goes on …

A spot of shopping with Mum in city, otherwise my parents are left to busy themselves as I attend appointments.

I'm loving that they return to my place and cook me dinner most nights.

Mum's Diary Note: Kelly is doing well; all specialists seem to be in place. We go back and forth to her apartment to help a bit.

I book Mum's and Dad's plane tickets home tonight, only three more days until they go. It's the catalyst for me to speed up my driving assessment—three hours of testing, yikes. I'm focused, and eager to pass so I can drive Mum and Dad to the airport in a few days' time. I feel good, I spend the first few hours of the assessment completing a physical and answering traffic scenarios on an iPad.

The OT assessor is quite thorough, and I realise I have not understood the enormity of my spinal cord and brain injuries. My strength, sensation, co-ordination, reaction time, vision and cognition are all assessed. Then I nervously head downstairs to enter a car fitted with a dual brake, just like when I was a teenager learning to drive. I'm nervous having an OT *and* a driving instructor watching my every move. I carefully navigate unfamiliar streets. The aim of the long session is to see how I cope concentrating and how I respond to traffic, due to my brain injury. And as I have reduced strength and shoulder range they're assessing if I may need to use a spinner knob on the steering wheel. Wow really, I'm not keen for any adaptations to my car, still subconsciously striving to just be 'normal', when realistically what is normal these days? If it means I have my independence and I can drive it shouldn't matter.

Building My New-Normal Life

Thankfully I pass, winning! I'm super proud of myself, but I'm soon gutted though when I share with them that my car is manual, not automatic like the car they tested me in. Not ideal considering my limited hand function, but hey, it's what I own. So next week I must drive again. It's probably for the best as driving Mum and Dad to the airport will be an emotional time. Besides, my car has a flat battery, urgh. Yet another thing to deal with.

Mum's Diary Note: Kevin and I are struggling with all sorts of emotions today.

The farewells begin with dinner at Carla's house, and the following day I take Mum and Dad for a nice lunch in Balmain, so nice to relax and sit outside a café in the sun. Quietly I cherish this moment reflecting on the past four months and the support I've received. I'm so thankful for them. Mum and I don't need to exchange our feelings, we turn and smile at each other knowing the love and special bond we have. ♥

A final afternoon tea at Jacqui's, knowing she is also appreciative and thankful for my parents. I'm sure we will have a lifelong friendship.

Monday 31st August 2020, Mum and Dad fly home. Not knowing when I'll see them again makes me feel ill, yet I know they must go home. Sadly, they must isolate for two weeks … I feel a forced rest will do them good.

Mum's Last Diary Note: Well, the day is here!!! Homeward bound. I am happy about it, but also scared to leave my beautiful daughter. I know she is strong and capable to cope on the path ahead as she has a great, supportive network of friends to help her, BUT they are not her Mum. I have spent so much time by her side these last four months that, though I am so blessed that we have her with us, it will take me a while to cope with this. Stay strong my beautiful girl. Love you always xxx

I find being at home quite lonely and, although I get by, it is an effort to look after myself. Constant juggling of appointments, the support workers are helpful but don't know how I like things done. It's quite demoralising and sad, but I don't share this with Mum as I need her to know that I am doing okay on my own. I must cope.

My love for cooking fades as I keep knocking and cutting my still-numb hands. I make multiple trips to get groceries as I'm unable to carry heavy bags upstairs. Fresh fruit and vegies are a must as I'm well aware good nutrition is key for my healing.

I find it difficult dealing with the chronic pain, stiffness, limited movement, constant fatigue and disinterest in things I previously found joy in. I struggle with brain fog daily, trying to prioritise my needs, rest and manage multiple therapy sessions.

Sleep is still uncomfortable: I can't turn onto my side, neuropathic pain in my right arm, metal in my left cheek, and my body is still feeling foreign to me. The urgency and frequency for bathroom visits impacts my enjoyment of normal outings, such as going to the shops. My anxiety is oh-so real.

Wow, how did I end up here? I sigh.

I'm, pleased to learn my parents are doing okay now they're safely back home, friends drop off groceries to them, my brother drives by with the kids waving to see Nanna and Papa and I'm thankful for Skype, seeing their faces and them mine. Mum has unpacked, washed, and cleaned everything. I suggest they do some lunges up and down the hall, as I appreciate that they're going a bit stir-crazy confined to their home. Luckily, they have a nice outside area with a garden to potter in.

Building My New-Normal Life

Normally a fun-loving and energetic person, I find my social life is constantly impacted by my injuries. My normal zest for life and adventure soon switches to me struggling with my emotions, being grumpy, uncertain of my capabilities, unable to attend late-night social events. I feel uncomfortable in large groups of people, especially if multiple conversations are occurring, and I'm constantly tired, drained by a life of constant pain and rehab. Enjoying a few wines is usually a big part of my social life, but that's now gone as alcohol consumption is advised against due to my TBI. Honestly, I don't really feel like it anyway.

Normal daily grooming activities are a challenge, I struggle to cut my fingernails, pluck my eyebrows, colour my own hair—just add them to the list of things which make me feel unlike myself.

I have a constant battle with my emotions: how does my boyfriend feel about me? My appearance has been affected by my injuries; my broken jaw means I now snore—it's so embarrassing. My speech is lisp-like, worsening when I tire; I stall to recall words and string them into a sentence, hoping they make sense. I feel horrible, I struggle to reconnect with friends on the same level as I had previously because my life is now consumed by rehab activities. I try not to dwell on the negative, nor let these things stop me socialising, they're no reason to not show up. It's my choice to make the best or worst of these situations, every obstacle and thought is either a stumbling block or a steppingstone. I'm taking one step at a time and I'm not giving up. It doesn't mean I don't feel all of the feels, I do and that's okay I tell myself. What else *can* I do?

Sadly, my designer jumpsuits are no longer practical for me to wear with urgent tendencies for the bathroom a regular occurrence for me, and buttons or zippers aren't my friends because of my limited hand movements. Cold weather affects me quite badly, so I mostly wear long-sleeve tops due to constant neuropathic pain in my right arm. I feel a sense of relief if my arm remains warm and covered. And I must juggle this with my body temperature being all over the shop, no doubt due to the impact to my spinal cord and nervous system. I yearn to wear my nice tops, but reducing my pain and being comfortable comes first.

My shoes need to be flat, because I'm at greater risk of tripping due to numbness in my feet, then add to that my lazy, weak ankles. No ripping up the dance floor for me. Disheartened, more things challenge me to get moving in the morning and out of the house. I want to wear my nice clothes and shoes, yet I must also be practical. Boring! To be honest, I don't have the energy to worry too much, I just want to get on with my day so gym pants and a top is often my attire, oh and my best crooked smile. 😊

Ugly nonslip bathmats, a chair in the shower, aids in my kitchen, are all constant reminders of my injuries. Simple daily tasks cause discomfort and pain: hanging out washing is cold and aggravates my neuropathic pain, holding and manoeuvering earrings is frustrating, and I often drop things as my hands are unable to grip things easily.

Constantly curious, yep sounds like I'm at work, but I'm thankful for this trait as I look into and try new therapies, seeking relief for my pain. Feldenkrais, Structural Integration Therapy, Lidocaine patches, InterX therapy, Psychologist EMDR (eye movement desensitization and reprocessing)—there's some really interesting stuff out there. It all comes with constant hope, disappointment, time, and a financial burden as iCare doesn't cover everything. I figure it out and weigh up the pros and cons, my constant drive and focus is to get better.

Building My New-Normal Life

At the peak of my rehab, I have ten appointments a week, clocking up seeing twenty-six different types of specialists over a six-month period. Managing my life of appointments constantly drains me, not to mention organising time to see my friends, my boyfriend, completing house duties, and simply resting. Life feels exhausting and monotonous, but I am still here.

I find a weekly planning chart on a random visit to Target. Voila! Instant visibility of my weekly activities makes it so much simpler to juggle my life and allow for recovery. Definitely a win.

That Morning: Piecing Things Together

Details about *that* morning slowly filter through to me via various people who were involved on that day.

How my emergency contact found out (thank goodness I carry an emergency contact card in my cycling wallet). To how she found my brother via LinkedIn, he shares the same name as her late pet rabbit. To how he had to go to the school where my mum works to tell her as she didn't answer her phone. To my workplace discovering why I was absent from my 9 am meeting, and finally to why my boyfriend's morning messages went unanswered. So many accounts of the morning are still unclear to me.

Amidst the pandemic and with limited flights, Mum and Dad were unable to get to me for two days. Leaving their three-bedroom house in Adelaide to stay in my two-bedroom apartment on the third floor in Sydney, travelling to and from hospital every day, navigating public transport—how horrible this made me feel. Their life on hold in a different state, and without friends and support, whilst worrying if their baby girl was going to live.

They must have experienced significant anxiety being unable to reach me for several days, then seeing me: hooked up to multiple machines in ICU, unconscious for six days whilst undergoing multiple lifesaving surgeries.

Talking To The Police

My phone rings all the time with 'no caller ID', due to the variety of people I am in contact with for my rehab activities. And today is no different as I answer the phone.

Constable XXX, it's the police. I gulp, they want to come and take my statement, my heart sinks, I panic, although I know I have done nothing wrong. There's always a 'but what if ...' It feels weird having them in my lounge room, especially as I'm no help. I'm still unable to recount events of that day, my only memory is of leaving my house early to ride and meeting Jacqui.

I'm told there is CCTV footage active in the intersection where I was hit, the driver is a young woman who will likely be charged, a court date set for January.

Jacqui forwarded me a letter the driver wrote, apologising. I wonder if the driver thought to do this or if her mum suggested it. The note says how sorry she is for her inattention that day.

She will never know the pain she has caused me or my family, however, she needs to live with the consequences of her actions and, no doubt, the impact of me going head-first into her windscreen. THUD! No one does these things deliberately. I'm appreciative of the note, a nice gesture all the same.

When my lawyer works on claiming compensation for my bike

and damaged property, I'm gutted to learn that the insurer applies such a high level of depreciation to everything. I'm astonished as my bike is only four months old and it was a big investment. Disheartened, I wonder how I'm meant to replace it all: kit, helmet, sunglasses—not to mention my bike. It's so unfair on top of everything else. Am I there yet? Am I even thinking I will get back and ride again …

A few weeks later Jacqui takes me to collect my bike from the police station, I'm surprised they're returning it to me. I'm surprised I even want to see it. We head inside, I don't think I really prepared myself for what I was about to see. The front wheel is bent in half, the tyre and tube hang separately, the front forks are broken, the left handlebar is in pieces and hanging loosely. All I can think is, wow, I survived this.

Surviving I am.

Some months later I drop my bike to the bike shop, not wanting the memory of it. I remove the lights, the drink bottle cages, and the saddle bag, advising them to do what they will with it, use it for spare parts.

Building My New-Normal Life

Picking up the remains of my bike from the police station

Back On The Bike

Seeing a Trauma Psychologist, both in and out of the hospital, was just one of the many services provided to me. In hospital I felt I was coping okay due to my devoted mother and amazing support network; so I didn't see this service as a priority for me.

Upon reflection, I was protected in hospital from a lot of life's challenges, enabling me to focus purely on myself and my rehabilitation. Once out of hospital, things changed dramatically as my reality set in.

Weekly sessions with my psychologist, amongst other appointments, soon become my new normal. I'm surprised how well my psychologist knows me. So well, in fact, about five months post my discharge from hospital she identifies how important cycling is to me. It is so much more than just a source of exercise; cycling keeps me physically and mentally fit, it's my social network, and it provides a sense of belonging: to a cycling club and the charity Tour de Cure. It was a *huge* part of my life.

I'm challenged by the idea of getting back on the bike, and this takes me by surprise. I'm still learning to walk and balance properly, so cycling hasn't even entered my mind. Fear immediately washes over me. But this is soon followed by the possibility and excitement of thinking about returning to the saddle, cycling with my friends, and being outdoors, feeling the fresh air on my face. The psychologist explains about engaging the help of a recreational therapist, and hearing her speak highly of a lady she knows, and has worked, with I agree. My journey to get back on the bike begins here.

The day soon comes for me to meet Amanda, the recreational therapist; I have no idea what to expect, but I know I want to try. My psychologist joins us in case I panic and need further support, which is silently comforting. We all meet at my local netball courts, the familiar surroundings being helpful. I freeze when I see an incumbent bike, designed to sit horizontally and close to the ground, shocked as it's bought out. Fortunately, I soon giggle as to me that isn't cycling, yet I appreciate that for some it is.

I do what I'm told, I sit in the seat, listen how to operate the bike, and then take off. I'm pleasantly surprised with the rush I feel as I ride around the netball courts. Before long I'm laughing and almost accidently flip it.

Real nerves kick in the following week when we meet again, this time with a flat bar bike. Balance is still a challenge for me and getting on an actual freestanding bike is confronting and a tad scary. Helmet on, even this feels weird as it isn't mine nor a light-weight one, sadly mine had to be thrown out. Yes, I know I'm being precious, it's all about the style, my cycling friends would understand, but it's the least of my worries really.

Can I balance? Can I actually ride again? Will my body be okay? What happens if I fall? Worse yet, if I hit my head?! So many thoughts, questions, and concerns go around in my mind.

My psychologist has opted not to join this time, reassuringly Amanda stands behind me like a kid who has just had the trainer wheels taken off their bike. I slowly find my bike legs and take off, pedalling slowly. The safety of the netball courts mean I can focus just on pedalling and staying upright.

"I'm doing it!" I yell, biggest smile ever on my face

Back On The Bike

Smiles all around are encouraging, what a great job Amanda has, I think. The next thing I know she places some cones down the length of the netball court and tells me to weave in and out of them.

Okay, bring it! With a renewed sense of confidence, energy, and enthusiasm off I go. Twisting and turning I weave around the cones up and down the netball court. So happy with myself, maybe a tad cocky, definitely a huge sense of achievement. I beam with happiness, noticeable by the sense of lightness within myself as I tackle the course.

Quietly it feels like I'm dreaming, I really can't believe I am back on a bike. A little over eight months ago I was hit by a car, I had multiple, major life-saving surgeries, I learned to walk again, and yet here I am back on my bike.

Amanda and I discuss what's next; I have never been big on setting goals, I usually thrive on jumping into the deep end, but I must pace myself, listen to my body, and go about things gradually, step-by-step. Luckily my patience is improving.

My homework before we meet next is to buy a new helmet— super confronting—and have my old road bike serviced. If I'm serious about returning to road cycling this is what needs to happen, because Amanda doesn't have a road bike for me to progress on to.

Just the thought of buying a new helmet creates a sickening feeling in my stomach. What if I invest a few hundred dollars and then I can't get back into road cycling? I'm not working, so my finances still play on my mind.

My passion for riding, my love for the sport, having time with friends, and adventures along the way is my 'why', so I embrace it and purchase a new helmet. It's scary yet exciting all at the same time.

My old bike is serviced and good to go, with two weeks passing I'm back at the netball courts ready. New helmet on, feels so much nicer to have my own. Sneakers on for now until I get comfortable and feel stable, then I will progress to clipping my bike shoes onto the pedals. A few deep breaths and off I spin. Slowly but surely, I navigate my way weaving around cones on the netball courts, smiling uncontrollably. Amanda, an absolute delight, cheers me on. Her smile and words of encouragement are all I need.

Amanda advises me that I should look at getting my handlebars raised a bit to allow for my shoulder pain. I'm relieved, this will be a minor modification, and no doubt an easy one for the boys at the bike shop to adjust for me. Subconsciously I just want to feel, and be viewed as, the same as others; yet at the same time I just want to ride.

Reflection: It's interesting that my own apprehension of being labelled with a disability drove some of me wanting my life to be the same, for me that represented being 'normal'. The reality is it will never be the same, people's abilities vary so broadly and mean so many different things. Old beliefs, even though they were not negative ones, sat uncomfortably with me. As a Senior Leader I have always operated with compassion and respect, strived to open people's eyes to capability, and operated with inclusivity, providing a variety of people with opportunity. It felt weird to think differently about myself, yet I yearned for my normal.

> *'The biggest thing is that for every one thing you can't do, there are 10,000 others you can. For every one idiot to give you a hard time,*

Back On The Bike

there are 10,000 others worth your time.'

Dylan Alcott

I now have a new appreciation of the world of disability and the different levels of ability that people can experience.

* * *

The next step is to ride the full circumference of the bay run, seven kilometres. Dodging children and walkers is a concern even though it's the middle of the day. Amanda and I complete this loop a few times over the coming weeks whilst I keep up my physio and fitness. I'm grateful for the luxury of being able to jump on my bike trainer set up in my spare room so I can continue to rebuild my strength. Ready to get back into my Lycra, I ask Amanda for our next session to be in Lane Cove National Park (LCNP). I am keen to put my cleats on, clip into my pedals and ride in the safe space of LCNP, cars not being permitted through until 9 am. I'm delighted when my cycling friend Ros, a registered nurse, has a late shift and joins us.

An awesome morning out, it feels quite surreal riding along the road, chatting just like old times. I'm so proud of myself to have come this far. It felt great to be back in Lycra, matching socks, matching hat, gloves—yep, it's a cycling thing, lol.

I begin driving the forty-five minutes from home to LCNP at least twice a week, as I feel comfortable there riding the four-kilometre length of road on my own. The 'no cars before 9 am' rule allows my mind to be at ease. Carrying my bike downstairs and lifting it onto the rack at the back of my car each day is a mission, however, it's amazing how I never think too much of it. I just get it done and drive to the park which has become my safe space, enabling me to do what I love outdoors in the fresh air.

Breaking Up With My Wheelchair

This is another form of therapy for me, the positive kind.

What I have learned: Find your 'why' for your exercise and rehabilitation activities, rather than go through the motions of mindless physio. Have the bigger picture front of mind, think about what you 'get to do.' Reframe your inner dialogue, remove anything negatively associated with these activities and get it done. Makes it so much more pleasant!

I don't love the early mornings, the drive, or the traffic, but once I'm in the park whizzing up and down the road, I become so alive and exhilarated I leave all my worries behind. This is like medicine for me, my WHY …

Building up to fifteen kilometres, to twenty kilometres, and even to thirty kilometres is an amazing achievement. I log I it all on Strava, an app used for tracking physical exercise that also incorporates social network features. I love seeing my progress, not to mention the kudos and encouragement from my followers. I'm still a long way away from my one-hundred-kilometre days, but it doesn't matter as I am back on my bike. I'm feeling incredibly grateful with the goals of further rebuilding my strength, getting back on the road, and cycling with my friends. My happy place.

Months of riding in the park follow, as well as rebuilding strength in the gym, and regaining my confidence and stability before I transition onto the road. I still have no memory of the accident, and that's a silent blessing. It soon feels like time to leave the safety of LCNP, so many butterflies, I'm feeling vulnerable and exposed, yet I know I need to push my worries aside and get on my bike and go. In many ways like a Nike advert, really—Just Do It!

Supportive friends make all the difference, I don't feel like a burden even though I'm much slower, and having Ros along helps to calm my mind and my fears. Thirty kilometres soon increases to fifty kilometres and now I'm riding three times a week, what a rush. It's all a bit surreal when I actually stop to think about it. I'm constantly amazed at what my body is achieving, and the continual encouragement from my friends spurs me on, more and more.

Reflection: It's important to reflect on the progress being made, big or small, as it is just that: progress. Be proud of these achievements. 'Progress over Perfection'. Keep moving yourself forward.

It's a challenge managing my neck and arm pain, plus I often need an urgent bathroom stop. My friends never complain, which is comforting, and they always make me aware of the routes we are cycling, and this reduces my anxiety of worrying about where I can stop.

I'm thankful for my tenacity, and my strong mind and body. Teamed with support from my cycling community, my passion for being out on the open road soon returns. It wasn't, and still isn't, easy. My arms and neck ache and my muscles are still rebuilding due to the damage to my spinal cord and nervous system, not to mention the constant neuropathic pain I feel. However, my love for the sport and the rush I receive from it drives me. It's weird too, as I find if I don't ride I become quite agitated. Cycling is medicine for me: the quality kind, my sanity. #dowhatyoulove

My First Fall

Covid-19 lock-down. Bugger! I must now remain within my local area; this means my cycling community is reduced to one person. Still not ready to cycle on my own, we plan a route and head out a few mornings a week. Trying to mix it up, and one morning a miscommunication on turning left or right sees us collide into one another.

I scream knowing I am going down; things are a blur I don't want to open my eyes, until I realise I can feel and move my body, hence I'm okay. The impact wasn't too harsh, just scratching my knee and arm, being covered by kit softens things a bit. My friend helps me off the road and away from traffic. We are followed by walkers who collect our bikes and ask if I am okay. Into shock I go, quickly becoming pale, I feel nauseous, trembling as the realisation washes over me and my nervous system: my body will never be the same again, I am forever fragile.

An off-duty doctor tends to me, elevating my legs on a log. In the meantime, my friend has rung her partner to come and help, and the doctor instructs him to grab a blanket out of his car. I'm now shivering. He takes our bikes to his car. Forever a cyclist, making sure the bikes are okay. I give him my shoes and helmet, it's amazing that in a crisis I think of these things as I lie there shaking.

All I really want to do is go to the bathroom, but unable to move I lie on the ground almost feeling paralysed. An ambulance soon arrives and I'm whisked off to emergency. I pray I don't defecate in my bike shorts whilst I'm in the ambulance, as I don't always have control over such things due to my SCI. An 'accident' would be super embarrassing. Bruised and sore, I feel a sense of comfort being reviewed by the paramedic, yet I feel uneasy about heading to emergency. I call my boyfriend once I'm stable inside the ambulance, being sure to say I'm okay after the fall, but that I'm heading to hospital to be checked out as a precaution. He agrees that the best thing for me is to be checked over thoroughly. Upon arrival at the hospital, I begin to feel less lightheaded, and I'm super relieved when I'm wheeled to the bathroom—I make it in time.

Thankfully, after a few hours I'm given the all-clear, my boyfriend picks me up and I head home. Bit shaken, but okay. I'm grateful for the kindness of the nurses in the Emergency Department.

Telling Mum that night is not easy, I opt to Skype her so she can actually see me and see that I'm alright. The beauty of technology. Wanting to keep moving forward and not let this set me back, I get back on my bike a few days later.

Over the following months there are many struggles due to my injuries, but also a lot of fun. I'm delighted to re-join my friends on smaller rides as it is so gratifying, and it provides immense joy. Some anxiety remains as I struggle to unzip my jersey quickly at toilet stops, fumbling with my hands, especially as the weather gets colder and I wear more layers to stay warm. Manual gearing and caliper brakes on my old bike prove troublesome as my dexterity and strength remain a challenge.

Although I ride, it's certainly not without self-doubt and voices in my head:

Can I keep up?

Can I climb the hills?

My First Fall

Climbing hills aggravates pain already in my tight chest, could I have a heart attack?!

What if I clip a wheel? Or worse yet, someone behind me clips my wheel and I go down?

Will my wheel slip out on road gravel, twigs, rocks (list goes on)?

What happens if I don't make it to a bathroom on time?

All of these thoughts, and more, are a constant in my head. It's my ability to acknowledge them, and then push past them, that enables me to focus on my 'drivers': why I am here, the social connection, the love of the sport, the sense of belonging, the fresh air, the *rush.* They all feed my mental and physical wellness. I push through the hard stuff, gaining momentum towards the good stuff. When I can, I always prefer to start my day with a ride, I feel better, I'm more positive, energised and ready to tackle the day.

Stretching, allowing my body the rest it needs post-ride, and refueling with nutritious foods are all important and a 'must' so I can recover well. Of course, I want to do it all again. Occasional massage is essential for me to release my tight muscles as I'm doing a lot to rebuild them, both on and off the road.

Returning To Adelaide And Visiting Mum

It's nearly Christmas and pandemic-mandated border restrictions have eased, so I'm delighted to be able to book a trip home to Adelaide and finally see my family. I'm really missing Mum and she is pretty excited to be seeing me too. The thought of flying scares me a bit, my body still feels foreign to me, and I'm unsure what harm the altitude might do. Feels silly, but I check with all of my therapists anyway, especially around my brain injury, best to calm my anxiety of concerns. Turns out I've nothing to worry about.

Seeing Mum at the airport is quite emotional, we've been apart now for almost five months. A quick hug only, as she has driven-through to collect me, and we head home. We sit for a long time that night catching up. Not that I say too much. It's difficult for me as, although I've improved a lot, I can see and sense Mum's loss. I'm still her daughter and always will be, however, I know she feels as though 'I'm not me'. This is quite hard for me to digest; I feel so uncomfortable and sick in the stomach because I feel the same way, but it's more real coming from my mother. This saddens me. My belief about myself post-injury is something I work on with my psychologist, as it sits uncomfortably with me.

My brother is coming around today with my niece and nephew, I can't wait to see them and show that Aunty Kel is doing okay. It must have been a tremendous shock for them learning of my accident, the traumatic injuries, and my hospital stay. Out they bound from the car and into my welcoming arms, the warmest of hugs everywhere. So good. Tears flow when I hug my brother, his solid support at the time of the accident reinforces how close a brother's and sister's bond can be. It's enlightening really as, although I would say we always got along living in different states, we don't usually chat a lot. This definitely changes our relationship for the better.

I talk to the kids inside, sharing more about my journey, conscious they're ten and twelve years-old. I burst into tears after a few minutes, my emotions overwhelming me as my story unfolds. We all hug, and I hold the space telling them how much I love them and miss them. We sit for some time, blessed to hold this emotional space.

The next day I catch up with Julie-Anne, an Adelaide-based cycling friend for coffee at the beach. She has ridden down to Glenelg with her three kids. I'm not sure how she knows about my accident, but it's most likely through other cycling friends. Not many people know about it, and it was definitely not something to post on socials. It's nice to share my story, receiving genuine compliments on how impressed she is with my recovery. I'm still not sure if the considerable progress I've made has fully sunk in, I'm lucky to be here and walking. I'm happy I can walk and talk and do things for myself. Hospital life is still all too real a memory for me.

Reflection: I can't recall exactly how I felt about going to Adelaide. I think I felt apprehensive as I struggled with being out of my own space and comfort zone, but my need to see my Mum and be

My First Fall

with her overrode this.

Travelling Solo

New Year's Eve is usually a bit of a doozy for me in Adelaide, however, the simple pleasure of being with my family at the beach followed by a barbecue in my brother's front yard is super fun, and a relaxing way to see the new year in.

A few days later I am meant to be flying to King Island to see Bex, one of my closest friends, again pushing myself outside of my comfort zone. Unfortunately, restrictions due to Covid-19 come into play and I accept a credit for my flights. Grr! Because it's a smaller airline, I must rebook for another time as the ticket is only relevant to King Island. Figuring out the logistics tests my brain as I need to rebook that flight, and now I need a flight back to Sydney.

I'm sad to say goodbye to everyone, yet I feel comforted in knowing I'm fine to fly and I'll see them again soon. Already talking about meeting Mum on the Gold Coast mid-year. We do something together every year for her birthday.

I'm delighted that I have sorted out all the rescheduled flights for King Island, and I rebook for February. The focus required to organise the logistics makes me a bit anxious, I'll need stop in Melbourne, then take a connecting flight to King Island. I check, and triple check, to make sure my flights all connect: right times and dates.

Turns out there was never any need for me to worry as it all goes smoothly, connecting flights and luggage a breeze. There waiting at the tiny airport when I land on the island is Bex, all smiles. We haven't seen each other in nearly a year, as she went to King Island to be with her family during the Covid-19 pandemic, and stayed there. I'm quite proud of myself for organising everything and making the trip happen. Knowing how important she is to me and wanting to visit her family and second home has driven this.

It's wonderful to meet her family and experience the island, everyone is very welcoming. My friends mean the world to me, and I know both she and I will remember this for a long time. Not to mention the fact we get bogged driving along the beach in some soft sand. Good times.

PART THREE:
Hero Skills

Meeting A Fellow Paraplegic

Nearly a year to the day after my accident I reach out to a fellow athlete, a motivational speaker. Someone I had been fortunate to spend time with—on and off the bike—in 2018 as part of several corporate events, while learning their inspirational story. A post on LinkedIn is what initially prompts me to reach out. Recalling his ability to overcome adversity spurs me on to send a message; fortunately we are already connected on LinkedIn.

The significance of why I want to reconnect with John Maclean? John is an incomplete paraplegic. I have a sudden yearn to talk to someone who has gone through something similar to me: most notably the enormity of living with a spinal cord injury, while also living with the constant determination of striving to be better.

I worry that John might not respond, as it has been a few years since we had last met. Amazingly, not only does he respond, but he invites me to catch up over lunch, conveniently we live quite close to one another. We follow this meeting up with a few rides and coffee afterwards.

This is exactly what I am seeking: an open and honest conversation with a like-minded individual who is also living with life-changing injuries. Someone who understands the mental and physical challenges, and the struggle they bring. I attempt to articulate what drives me, *why* I keep challenging myself. *Why* I push myself at physio, with the exercise physiologists, and the recreational therapist. *Why* I challenge myself in life, such as flying to see my friend on King Island, and also generally day-to-day.

Our conversations enlighten me, inspire me further, and help me to realise that anything really is possible. I was already seeing the results from working hard, but now I understood—although I have not verbalised it—that it was *my* way: constantly moving forward in the hope to be seen as an equal. He hit the nail on the head. Wow! That's it. I just wanted to be viewed and treated as an equal, to be 'normal' again. I wanted all the pain I had suffered, and was still suffering, and all the anguish I had caused others, to disappear.

But really, I ask myself, what does 'to be seen as an equal' represent? What was I truly hoping for?

'Embrace Change'—strengthens, challenges, and allows us to become who we want to be.

My desire to be seen as an equal, is feeling all-too real, and it is exciting that I have now voiced it, yet deep down I know I will have to build a *new normal*. And I would be in charge of creating it.

Coping with life out of hospital and working towards my new normal is a constant battle. Dealing with persistent fatigue means that most days the struggle is real. I don't have any idea of what I'd like my new normal to look like, especially as rehab activities take up most of my time. Thoughts of returning to work have entered my mind, but I am just not sure where or how I'd fit it in. Fortunately, there is no pressure from my employer.

Meeting A Fellow Paraplegic

Dealing with lawyers and iCare, understanding what I am entitled to, and what my future will look like, is overwhelming. It causes me a great deal of anxiety, and as I'm a single female there are so many unknowns for me. I am receiving eighty per cent of my salary, I am grateful for this, and I make it work.

I constantly research, and talk to my therapists, I am curious about what other therapies I can try, not just for my physical recovery, but for my brain and my overall wellness too. I am flabbergasted when I am told that I would see improvements in my brain function for three years or more post-injury due to my traumatic brain injury. Such a lengthy recovery.

Who Am I: Struggling With My Identity

I often find myself lingering when looking at myself in the mirror, I know it's me staring back, yet at the same time it's *not* me. I'm grateful to have my own teeth, yet I wish they were straighter, along with my overall smile. I have a droopy lip and some residual numbness from the deep cut to my chin, and I stutter at times when I talk. My right cheek is flatter than usual as a result of my broken jaw, a scar on my outer right eye causes creases when I smile.

They are all little things but they feel big to me and, with the exception of my mother, I'm the only one who really notices them. Embracing the new me is easier said than done. Yearning for what was, especially when capturing new memories and seeing photos of myself, leaves me with a feeling of sadness.

Questions swirl around my head. I ponder …

Who am I?

Who will I now become?

Who, and What, do I *want* to be?

Breaking Up With My Wheelchair

What will my future hold?

For all my determination, courage, strength and resilience, I've shown I still falter, have down days, get angry, and wonder 'why me'. There are the occasional tears of sadness, and more often there's exhaustion as I tackle each day. Like the spin cycle of a washing machine or a hamster on a wheel, wondering when things might improve and when the spinning will slow down, better yet … cease. Like all rides, I want it to end, get off, it would be nice if the spinning just stopped.

I remain open-minded about varying approaches with my Trauma Psychologist, as I receive so much value in our weekly sessions. It's nearly one year on, and even with such growth, her understanding of me continues to amaze me. This type of support—insights into my thoughts and feelings—helps to normalise what I'm experiencing as I navigate my life and my feelings towards myself and try build my new normal.

My lack of confidence impacts my life enormously, how I see myself and show up, especially now that I'm not working. Constant reminders of my accident can be as little as when I'm washing my face, feeling my hard cheekbones now held together with metal plates. This is in addition to other reminders, like the permanent neuropathic pain in my right arm and my stiff, sore neck.

The orthodontist has now given the all-clear for my braces, and this brings some excitement as *finally* my bite and smile will hopefully be fixed. Yet, having had braces when I was fifteen years old, I'm apprehensive about the process, and the potential discomfort and pain. Having braces at forty-three years of age feels embarrassing, not to mention that it's a huge inconvenience.

Who Am I: Struggling With My Identity

Urgh! The pain from keeping my mouth open for hours whilst the braces are fitted. Although I'm aware that braces are for any age, I don't want them, nor do I feel comfortable with them. It's just another reminder, and more discomfort that I need to cope with. Gets worse when I try to eat, everything sticking in my braces, hooks grip and rip my cheeks, and inside my lips. OUCH! It's super frustrating, but one must persevere as an improved smile and chewing function is in my future, near future.

Things gradually begin to shift for me as I work on myself, reflect, and create a new perspective on life. What's now important to me continues to shift: who I spend time with, and where and who I give my energy to, whilst trying to remain positive around what I 'get to do', as opposed to what I'm missing out on. Even so, that one-hundred-kilometre ride is still on my mind, still a future goal of mine.

My strong mind and body are constantly surprising me with what I can achieve. I realise it's also a matter of time and patience: time to heal, and patience when responding to what happens to me.

Although I'm not at work, the 'Art of The Possible' saying we have within the technology space feels so true for me at this moment. My struggle now is to embrace all that I'm becoming and focus on the new me, as opposed to mourning for the old me. Thinking what is possible if I just try ...

Life goes on, weeks full of therapy, trying varying treatments such as Feldenkrais, and InterX,—a non-invasive electrical stimulation to communicate with the central nervous system. So hoping multiple sessions with this would help relieve the constant sense of pressure I have in my chest, which is often crippling when I walk. It feels like someone has their boot on my chest causing a heavy tightness and discomfort.

Some weeks previously I completed a lung capacity test, locked in what looked like an old telephone booth, and it showed that my lungs were fine.

I keep trying and hoping. Add to the list structural integration therapy, acupuncture, and a psychologist performing Eye Movement Desensitization and Reprocessing (EMDR) therapy. EMDR uses eye movements to change the way a memory is stored in the brain, allowing you to process it. Surprising really, allowing myself to embrace this type of therapy helped me to process a lot of the self-belief I had as a result of my mum verbalising, 'I'm not me'. Her grief and adjusted view of me linked in with what I now believed about myself, however, hearing it out aloud hit me quite hard.

Therapy isn't easy, it's often confronting, uncomfortable and hard work, however, there are rewards if you can be vulnerable, honest with yourself, and embrace the process.

Reflection: I truly believe the support I received had a positive effect on me and my mental wellbeing for some time. There was always a sense of lightness after my sessions.

The sessions vary depending on the level of my chronic pain, how my day has been, and whether I commit to the session or not. I receive the most benefit on the days I am most vulnerable, with the pain in my chest easing accordingly.

A trip to the Gold Coast sees me seek out Ken Wares to further understand the science of NeuroPhysics Therapy, which contains some insightful and amazing exercise-based rehabilitation programs. It is overwhelming and I opt to continue with what I have access to locally, knowing that I can revisit the program in the future.

Learning what is available keeps driving me, I am constantly curious; 'knowledge is power' as they say. I am grateful just knowing that there are other options available to try.

Reading *The Brain That Changes Itself* by Norman Doidge MD, blew my mind. It explains how the brain is capable of undergoing change in response to experience, learning, and stimulation. Phenomenal. Definitely a motivator. The need to remain 'forever a student' still rings true even though, in my leadership role, I had been a teacher.

I work with a speech pathologist to correct difficulties I have speaking clearly. My compromised brain-mouth connection, and my increasing anxiety are not helping my stutter. Needing to do the work, I consciously start using my brain more to assist with its healing. It's amazing what games, and daily challenges amongst others, you can find on your phone. I also begin to socialise and network more, needing to reconnect and expose myself to more stimulating interactions. My need to return to work is on the horizon, so improving my communication skills and restoring cognitive function is vital.

I'm now riding about fifty kilometres per session and I'm loving it. My cycling community are the most amazing, supportive, and encouraging bunch of people. The way I feel when I'm out on the open road is indescribable, such a rush and a sense of freedom. The rides are a daily booster reminding me of what I get to do, as opposed to what I don't.

Although the rides are fun, they remain quite taxing on my body, team this with constantly pushing myself at the gym and it leaves me exhausted. I must diligently manage my body: stretching, relaxing, and recovering, not to mention eating well too. It's no easy journey, however, I continue to try multiple therapies hoping to restore my body. I'm conscious that the injuries from my crash will remain with me for life, so I do my best to manage my recovery daily.

Having always enjoyed and experienced relief from massages I am keen to give them another go post-injury. At the same time, I'm terrified that any pressure applied in the wrong place could compromise the metal structure in my neck. Although these fixtures are strong and the surgeon has reassured me it's okay, I'm mindful of his advice, "Don't let the masseuse apply pressure directly over the scar," and it will be fine. I can't help but have feelings of trepidation, thinking the worst, that I will be further damaged.

It's very clichéd, but I feel the fear and do it anyway. It's all about how we respond to our fears and what life presents us, so I proceed. Having faced so much worse I acknowledge my fears, yet I also look at the potential positives, hopeful for some relief in my tight shoulders, back, and neck muscles. Some relief from my persistent headaches would be a welcome change too. I share my injuries and concerns with the masseuse prior to them starting, delighted it's no problem and they're super calm. I lie face-down, warm hands with oil smooth over me and within minutes I relax into it, sooooo goooood!

Pelvic physio is next, which includes conducting an internal examination. No surprise, it's super uncomfortable, and even more so when my hip flexor muscles are released internally. Ouch! It's so excruciatingly painful that tears slide down my cheeks. Needles are inserted in my neck and in between my ribs to release opposing tight muscles, pulling every which way which causes various difficulties. I follow up with a lot of at-home exercises, twisting and turning to try to keep my ribs open and to reduce the pressure I feel. It's constant, always something

Who Am I: Struggling With My Identity

somewhere, my poor body.

Although I'm quite active, other parts of my life are impacted because of my physical limitations. I'm no longer agile or quick to do things like I used to, I now have a minimised ability to run, and I need to be cautious at the beach so I'm not taken by the waves. My days of cartwheels along the sand with my niece are definitely over.

The injuries from my crash will likely impact, or even impair, me for rest of my life. Who knows what the long-term effects could look like? Pain and suffering, arthritis, challenges with my brain. Not wanting to live in a bubble of 'maybes' or 'what ifs' I try not worry about the unknown and concentrate on enjoying my life.

Enjoy life—I do my best.

I'm asked to support the SA (South Australia) Discovery Tour with charity Tour De Cure in 2021. Raising money for cancer research lights up my world. Having successfully ridden a similar three-day tour in 2019, I knew I wasn't up for the ride, however, being a part of the support crew was something I could absolutely do. With friends participating, it made it all the more special to be involved, to contribute, and to form part of this amazing community. The goodness kept on coming when my friend, Tash, shared that she had sorted my fundraising requirement. It was the kindest gesture, removing what could have been a stressful obstacle to being involved. The excitement in the lead up, and feeling a part of the team, was the biggest boost to my confidence. I felt so included and valued as a support person in the accompanying cars, keeping everyone safe as they rode.

Some concern did wash over me as to whether I could survive the whole day, maintain my focus and control any urgency for the bathroom outside of stops. I know I joke about it, but sadly it's my reality that the effects of my brain injury and neurogenic bladder cause me anxiety. Couldn't let that stop me though. #livelife

The entire experience will remain with me forever. The generosity from other people, and being included at this point in my recovery, immensely raised my spirits and my feeling of being valued.

Upon reflection, it also showed me what I was capable of: surviving the three big days on the road, up early, responsible for certain jobs, all whilst keeping us on the correct route and encouraging those who were cycling.

Earning an 'Achieving' jersey on the awards night leaves me beaming; it's wonderful how being supported and belonging to a purposeful, friendly community can leave you feeling so positive and on top of the world. The icing on the cake is the tour taking place in Adelaide. Knowing most of my cycling friends, Mum is delighted to see them again, to wish them all well, and wave them off at the start line. So nice to be able to include her in this.

My sense of purpose, the realisation that life goes on—albeit looking a bit differently—and that it can still be enjoyed while creating new experiences, is renewed after these three days. The ability to look at things through a fresh, new lens, and allowing change to happen, combined with being around quality friends reinvigorates me. I also feel an enormous sense of pride and triumph as I drive into the winery at the completion of the three-day tour. All my family are there, including my brother, his partner, my niece and nephew, and Mum and Dad, all smiles clapping the riders in. I did it, I'm proud of myself and hopefully I have showed them that I am, and will be, okay.

I may not have ridden in the race, but I still felt like a winner while hugging my family and enjoying the celebrations with everyone at the beautiful surrounds in McLaren Vale.

This feeling of belonging continues when a month later my friends invite me for a cycling long weekend in Mudgee. Unable to complete the 120-kilometre-long local event, I focus instead on what 'I got to do' being their support and cheerleader, waving them over the finishing line, and joining in the festivities. A few smaller local rides provide me with the same rush, being out on the open road early, and exploring Mudgee and surrounds with my friends is unreal. My sense of adventure and enjoyment, whilst spinning, was the best feeling ever.

Unfortunately, things in life aren't always as we would like them or plan them to be. I feel that my ability to adapt to my environment and the opportunities presented—or even those I seek out—helps expedite my recovery. Remaining focused and positive and changing my dialogue to focus on what 'I get to do' helps. Things don't always look the same and often they're not ideal, but that's okay.

OMG!! First Anniversary Already

It's now been a year since that life-changing day.

I'm keen to ride with Jacqui, however, unfortunately this isn't an option as she is recovering from multiple fractures in her pelvis. Yikes, yep, you guessed it—a cycling accident.

Instead, we decide to head to Manly for a swim in the local pool, followed by breakfast. Although we don't see the sun rise, it is nice to take the time to hang out together, embrace our friendship, and enjoy a coffee and breakfast in the sunshine. I'm grateful for the strong women in my life, me their cheerleader and them mine. Supporting and celebrating each other. It's great for the soul.

We don't talk about *that* day; we don't need to.

Going from strength to strength, my friends recognise my increasing abilities on the bike, and I'm delighted to be invited to ride to Palm Beach. My favourite ride clocking up seventy-five kilometres would be a stretch, and my biggest since my accident, but I'm super keen. My head and heart are in. Amazing how support and encouragement from friends lifts you. I wouldn't say there's good conversation out on the open road, LOL, but there is a lot of humour and simply the united love of cycling together and catching up. Oh, and the coffee at Palm Beach, of course.

I'm shattered for the next three days, but this doesn't bother me too much, knowing that I'd ridden the seventy-five kilometres at a reasonable pace with my friends just over a year on from my accident. Phenomenal, what an achievement! That 100-kilometre dream goal is well within my sights.

Naturally, the next thing to do is invest in a new bike, right?

As a cyclist, 'new bike day' is super exciting as it generally doesn't come around that often. I have only ever experienced the rush once before, investing in a new bike just before my accident, so this is massive for me. I have been struggling with my old bike due to the calliper breaks requiring me to squeeze the levers tightly, aggravating the weakness in my hands. Hence, I'm keen to upgrade to a much lighter bike with electronic shifting and disc brakes for easier, softer breaking, much nicer and safer for my hands. It also means a smoother ride, plus it's safer in general for me as I am now going longer distances, so I'm out on the road for extended periods of time.

I spend some time researching new bikes and talking to the guy at the bike shop—who had assisted with modifying my old bike—to understand the different geometry of bikes available to me. A few models are shared with me, and he explains why each would be suitable across varying price ranges. Still amidst the Covid-19 pandemic, the availability of bikes is limited. Investing in a new bike is in my thoughts for weeks; scared, yet excited. This step forward represents so many things for me. Fortunately, I don't have to deliberate for too long. I receive a call just two weeks later advising me there is only one Pinarello in my size left.

OMG!! First Anniversary Already

My unwavering determination to rebuild took me from day one cycling around that netball court, to now riding on the open road again, and climbing hills. Riding is my therapy, my sanity, it is *who* I am. Deposit paid, done. The Pinarello Prince will be here in ten days, arriving from Melbourne.

I have to pinch myself. I am very happy with my decision, it is what I deserve, my reward for all the hard work. Feels amazing.

A few weeks later I head to the bike shop, and the stealthy black Prince is set up for me, a bike fit with minor adjustments to accommodate my needs. It's a beauty, Wow! I feel pretty special the next day riding the Prince, it is so smooth and easy on my hands, changing gears at the touch of a button, and braking is similar. Full approval from my cycling buddies.

Reflection: To this day I feel so lucky to be able to cycle. I know I did the hard yards, and I still do them, always pushing myself and working harder. Sometimes a surreal feeling will wash over me, to be back on my bike out on the open road cycling around Sydney is my WHY.

Christmas brings about the time to assess the year ahead and focus on what's important. My life has changed so much, and as a result, so too does the way I think, feel, and plan for my future. I know I'm getting stronger when I deliberate making the heartbreaking decision to call off my relationship with my boyfriend. We aren't wanting the same things, nor are we heading in the same direction. I've gone through so much and consequently I want so much more out of my life. He's not a bad person, and he's been so supportive, but that isn't reason enough for me to remain in the relationship. It brings me further feelings of despair as it's likely my last hope to have a family; I'm nearing forty-four years of age and I'm about to be single again.

These thoughts remain with me over Christmas. Fortunately, I borrow Julie-Anne's spare bike and enjoy several rides with her and friends. Borrowing Julie-Anne's spare bike enables me to have this much-needed time out, which is my saviour. I feel blessed by her friendship, and I am *so* grateful for it. Cycling truly is my sanity.

I end my three-year relationship in January 2022.

Returning To Work

In the back of my mind is my job; I have always been passionate about educating young talent. Designing and implementing programs that supported the needs of the business and the students' transition from university into the corporate workforce, then seeing them shine and achieve, made for a gratifying leadership role. My accident has changed all that, especially around my priorities and what is important to me.

The focus is now on me and my healing, although I remain in touch with work, and I am grateful to feel no pressure from them to return. When I'm ready they're fully supportive of a gradual transition. And I can't help but feel like I owe it to them to try.

I am fortunate to have access to a vocational specialist who provides support in this transition back to work, and maps out a Return-to-Work (RTW) plan. These consultations are quite draining for me, I keep hoping and thinking I am ready to return to work, but truthfully, I'm not. I'm juggling three gym sessions a week, plus physio, occupational therapy for my hands, Pilates, and I now ride two weekday mornings. Add to that, seeing my psychologist, dealing with lawyers and the insurance company amongst other ad hoc appointments, doing grocery shopping, cooking for myself—it is too much. I struggle to sit still and focus at the best of times when I'm reading or doing life admin. How will I function and apply myself at work?

I undergo four hours of cognitive testing, completing a comprehensive neuropsychological assessment because of my TBI. The evaluation assesses my abilities such as, concentration, speed of thinking, general intellect, language functioning, new learning and memory, plus higher-level thinking skills including problem solving, reasoning and planning, and organisation. Sigh. All the skills I need, if I am to successfully operate at a senior level again, are impacted.

Eager to try and test myself within a safe space, I start working two mornings a week, Mondays and Wednesdays, allowing for a rest day in between. It is difficult going from being a high-functioning specialist designing and managing Talent Programs to now struggling to concentrate on simple tasks. And with no real clarity of role or responsibilities I feel lost. This begins to impact my mental health, and with no real sense of purpose I become restless. I have difficulty focusing and sitting still, and I experience even more pain in my hands as I type. The headaches don't help either, and consequently I often mix up my words as I attempt to speak in a more professional manner.

On top of my personal challenges, the company I work for has changed dramatically due to the impact of the Covid-19 pandemic: I have a new manager and many of my stakeholders are now gone. This challenges me even further; I have to relearn the business, build rapport with new stakeholders, and navigate the ever-changing corporate landscape.

There are a lot of emotions as the weeks go on, especially frustration with myself while trying to understand the business, while struggling with my purpose, and while trying to operate within a completely different space. I add to my anxiety wondering how I make a difference two mornings a week, and especially a positive impact like I used to. I miss working closely with the business and driving new initiatives; this is what gets me excited.

It's all-consuming, and I suffer with mental fatigue because of the constant juggling of everything, the uncertainty, and not knowing what is happening from a legal perspective. More than anything I want that part of my life over.

* * *

Reflection: I've come to realise since this life-changing event that I'm comfortable sharing my story and embracing all my positive qualities, whilst acknowledging my not-so-good qualities. Sometimes I function on 5G, at other times maybe only 2G. I've managed to get this far, and I *will* keep moving forwards. Unfortunately, I'm not in the minority when it comes to living with trauma and life-changing injuries. Sadly, I have read many stories, listened to many a podcast, and I have taken inspiration from all of them. I just hope that sharing my story provides some inspiration, or at least hope, to others.

Something I came across on LinkedIn particularly resonated with me due to its positive spin to keep progressing, keep moving forward:

>**FAIL** = **F**irst **A**ttempt **I**n **L**earning
>
>**END** is not the end, in fact = **E**ffort **N**ever **D**ies
>
>**NO,** if you get NO as an answer, remember NO = **N**ext **O**pportunity

All valuable advice, regardless of any individual circumstances, in a life where we are forever a student *and* a teacher. With the world, technology, and us as humans, constantly changing we need to evolve and grow with it.

* * *

I continue to do the best I can, seeking feedback and trying my hand at various projects, whilst sharing my feelings and struggles with my psychologist. Life will improve, my brain will heal, my fatigue will lessen and become more manageable. I just have to keep doing the hard work whilst allowing for my rest days.

So, I listen to my body and do my best.

The Elusive 100km!

The Jindabyne training camp with the Cammeray Roadies, my cycling club, was sure to be a fun, few days away. Six adults, four dogs, and a whole lot of energy, enthusiasm, coffee, and Lycra in a share house. Fun times. I have missed these travel adventures.

Dead Horse Gap, Charlotte Pass, Berridale for coffee, and a few local spins. Wowsers! A few days full-on, a lot of climbing, exhilaration when reaching the peaks, and positive self-talk around spinning: keep the wheels turning, you will get there. Ros, my saviour once again, talks me up the climbs. My understanding of my body is certainly growing. I kindly tell Ros to make her way home with the others, sensing I would be slow and weary after tackling the climb to Dead Horse Gap.

Halfway down I make the tough decision to call Ros's partner to see if he can pick me up. He had driven to Thredbo and joined us for coffee, so I knew he wasn't far behind. Thankfully he answers my call, and happily picks me up. I'm comfortable with my decision, pleased I listen to my body. So, it's home, a protein shake and a rest before the rest of the festivities.

A few weeks later Saturday begins like any other, checking who is keen to ride, confirming what route we want to do, checking the weather is good, generally full of excitement and enthusiasm to be out with the crew. The TDC (Tour de Cure) are always a fantastic bunch to ride with due to their standards around etiquette and safety followed by riders across all capabilities, hence, I always feel safe riding in these pelotons.

It's comforting to know the ride leaders know of my injuries, but don't make a fuss; encouragement is customary amongst all riders with varying fitness levels across the pelotons. Because it's a ride to raise money for cancer research, everyone has the same sense of joy for riding, and kindness, in common.

Today is a reasonable distance, setting out from Neutral Bay to tackle Brooklyn, where we refuel and enjoy a coffee at a cafe by the water before heading home via Bobbin Head, and then back to Neutral Bay.

My elusive one hundred kilometres wasn't even in my thoughts, but upon returning to Neutral Bay my computer shows ninety-six kilometres ridden. Ros turns to me and asks if I have completed a one-hundred-kilometre ride since my accident. Stunned, I'm sure my blank face tells her I haven't. As I ride with her most days I have a sneaky suspicion she knows this.

Before I know it, Ros has yelled out to the ride leaders letting them know we'd be back as we were doing a further four kilometres to round our ride up to one hundred kilometres. A few cheers are heard, "Go Kell!" as we ride off. It all happens so fast that I am speechless for a moment, then I soon realise what is happening and, smiling my biggest smile ever and laughing with Ros, we take off. In search of the flattest route, we ride down the main road and back around the block.

Immense joy, a sense of achievement, and pure happiness fills me inside when my Wahoo, a very appropriate name for my cycling computer, soon clicks one hundred kilometres. I have achieved my biggest goal yet. As we pedal back to join everyone,

The Elusive 100km

I'm sure I am bursting with elation and I'm all smiles, thankful to Ros for recognising and valuing what completing one hundred kilometres represents for me. Especially as I am considering joining my friends cycling overseas for three weeks. Strength-to-strength riding really is possible for me.

So chuffed with the one hundred kilometres, the gals and I did it all again a few days later riding out to Kurnell, a much flatter route though. #backinthegame

Some might say it's crazy, but I feel lucky to be able to do what I love. It's taken me a while to verbalise it, but I'm worth it, I've worked tirelessly to get here.

My concerns regarding my ability, and my trepidation about not being strong enough are now a distant thought. I can, I *will*—end of story.

QOM—Queen Of the Mountain!

Second Anniversary: #dowhatyoulove

Navigating the roads of Sydney with my friends for months now, my love and continued enjoyment of cycling sees me eventually build up enough courage to ride from home solo. My heart has a constant sinking feeling, and I doubt it will ever go away. I'm hyper-alert and constantly wary of the traffic, but my sense of freedom overrides my fear. I set off alone, just me, my bike, the open road, and a smile on my face. Proud of what I have achieved, and continue to achieve. #dowhatyoulove

It feels so good to work through these fears and be able to commute from home on my bike to join others for rides. Driving is an option, however, it's much easier to get up and go on my bike and ride from home. Not that I'll ever be 'normal', but this definitely signifies some normality for me, more importantly it represents regaining my independence and pre-injury life activities.

France, Italy, and Spain. Some of my cycling friends are planning a trip overseas and ask me if I'd like to join. Could I?

I loved a similar trip we did in 2019. So many considerations swirl around my head. How will my body respond to a long-haul flight?

What happens if I have an accident overseas? How will I dismantle, pack, and unpack my bike?

I work through all these worries, and more, grateful that my friends are supportive and happy to help me with things like the mechanics. I was never particularly mechanics-savvy pre-accident anyway.

Steph, my friend who lives in France, recommends I use a backpack for my clothes so my hands will be free to manoeuvre my bike bag, as we will be taking a train to Italy. This proves to be the best advice, as I already struggle with my hand strength and dexterity, and everyone else will be managing their bikes and luggage so I need be as self-sufficient as I can be. I'm keen not to be a burden.

I'm silently happy that Ros, my nurse friend, will be joining us; I know I can confide in her if anything is going on for me. Her caring nature and ability to check on me without making a fuss is such a comfort.

Travel insurance is a must, but with research comes the realisation that it's quite costly for me, the need to acknowledge pre-existing injuries is a necessity. I think of Mum, and it's a no-brainer, plus it will put my mind at ease. Ahh, responsible adulting.

Say 'YES.' It's amazing when you unpack everything to make sense of things what you can make happen.

A trial packing up of my new bike to visit a friend in Brisbane is a good practice run, sorting out a few challenges with the dismantling of my bike. Disappointingly it rains all weekend and we don't even get to cycle. Ahh, the joys.

The countdown is on, I can't believe that nearly two years ago I

Second Anniversary: #dowhatyoulove

was hit by a car, in ICU having undergone multiple surgeries to save my life, and was having to learn to walk again.

Here I am packed and ready to go, it's quite surreal, but I'm super excited and a little bit anxious with so many unknowns and 'what ifs?' I won't put my life on hold because of a 'what if'. I have done all of my due diligence, including speaking to my specialists, and am as prepared as I can be.

Let's go, gals!

The flights are fine, but jet lag is a killer; I'm managing fatigue, and my bodily functions are all messed up, so I'm grateful for a few days in the comfort of Steph's place in France. The best medicine is easing into it, a few easy rides enjoying the local countryside, local food, and some relaxation before heading on to Italy.

Love Italy! I've visited before, and this time I'm comfortable because I'm with my friends, which makes it easier to manage my anxiety. We're staying at the *Garda Bike Hotel* in Lake Garda, where I know one of the owners. This brings a sense of excitement and familiarity, plus we're surrounded by likeminded people all there for the love of cycling. I'm so fortunate to be here.

Daily rides are quite casual, we are in Italy after all, stopping for coffee or gelato in little towns as we take in the sights. I am conscious to fuel, hydrate, and rest appropriately. I also enjoy a cold dip in the pool daily, it's cool, refreshing, and good for my body at the end of each day's ride.

What an epic way to celebrate all that I've achieved in the two years since my accident: being in Italy cycling with friends. Aww … yay for my cheerleaders, both on and off the bike. Thanks ladies.

On a ferry travelling with our bikes across Lake Garda, I take a moment to stare out over the crystal blue water, it shimmers brightly. It's difficult to digest how far I've come, so I sit in the moment, smiling, proud of myself for continually looking ahead and moving forward. Being brave and living my life, enjoying what I love and celebrating what I get to do— for it's me who is steering my ship and in control of my greatness.

On the ferry at Lake Garda

I breathe in the fresh sea air, my body loves the heat, it even thrives on it.

Our trip continues for another six days onto Spain, to the town of Girona, filled with more cycling adventures, amazing food, and lots of laughs.

This trip shows me just how strong I am; my tenacity, my sense of adventure, my drive and ability to keep moving forward, all strengthening my self-belief.

Dip your toe in the water, be courageous and try—you might just surprise yourself!

Reflection: To this day when I look at the photos, reminiscing about the trip, our adventures and what I achieved, it amazes me and fills me with joy. The body's ability to perform, and

Second Anniversary: #dowhatyoulove

constantly testing one's limits all whilst seeking out the next adventure; the open road ahead fills my cup and brings me a sense of calm. *This* is why I ride. #dowhatyoulove

Kicking Goals

LOVE. I am unsure whether I am ready, but I know I want to find someone to share my life with, so I decide to give online dating a go. Urgh! My stomach churns at the thought of endless scrolling, swiping, and meaningless conversations. But what other way is there? Thankfully, I have experienced online dating before and have my strategies.

I have good and bad dates, however, knowing this is to be expected helps prepare me mentally for the rollercoaster of ups and downs, conscious that I need to go through the motions. Fortunately, I meet some nice people and have some quality conversations and laughs, whilst keeping meet-ups simple with a walk or coffee, so I don't find it too tiring.

Slowly my confidence builds, I can do this, although it is a challenge answering the 'what do you do for work' questions. I talk all of this through with my psychologist, and shift my mindset to a place I am comfortable with when discussing my work and when it feels right to share the details of my accident and resulting injuries, inclusive of my change of lifestyle. A lot of my insecurities around the way I look and speak, and my life in general, are in my head, and it is a challenge to process this and adjust my thinking accordingly.

Sharing my accident with someone I don't know is quite a sensitive topic. Imagine meeting someone new, trying to build a foundation of trust, and then ... dropping that bombshell! Having someone understand the enormity and impact of my injuries on my life is difficult, especially as I look quite normal. Depending on the individual, their personality, and how I feel about them, dictates when and what I share. This works best for me, and it also quickly shows who is ready for a relationship and genuinely wants a life partner.

I entertain the apps on and off over an eight-month period, trying to mix it up and have fun with it, whilst rediscovering myself slowly and gently.

It's Christmas time, so I return to Adelaide again and, although I have matched with some people, I decide to let it be. Besides, most people are spending time with their families.

'Ping!' Adrian messages me; we connected about a week before, but he is only replying now. Funny and engaging, his messages immediately get my attention. We exchange numbers a few days later: chatting, laughing, and discovering a similar sense of humour makes it easy to connect. I share that I am in Adelaide for Christmas with family and uncover that he is also from Adelaide. Too funny. We further discover that we had both moved to Sydney about a year apart over twenty years ago.

Good banter, quality conversation and texts continue over the next week, easy, just the way I felt it should be. We meet up when I return to Sydney in the new year, we do a casual walk around the local bay, learning that we live within five kilometres of each other. We do the same walk the following day, not once struggling for conversation, even if some Adelaide bogan-slang jokes came about.

Our close proximity to one another makes catching up easy, meeting friends in the local suburb of Balmain is a quick indicator he is serious, no playing games here, which is brilliant. Our common interests of exercise, travel, and even cooking makes for a nice foundation of activities. Some serious competition in the kitchen and a passion for barbecues impresses me—he has four!

Spending time together feels comfortable, his sweet and caring nature makes it easy for me to share my story with him when the time feels right. Knowing it doesn't faze him is reassuring. Now that's adulting for you, people!

My independence is appealing to him, he likes that I have my cycling, as he enjoys his AFL and cricket. This is a relief, as I continue to get up early a few mornings a week to meet my friends and join club rides. I am actually increasing my training distances, having signed up for the 125-kilometre Mudgee Classic.

Yikes, what am I doing? As always, if I don't try I won't know. A few friends and some people from my cycling club are heading to Mudgee for the weekend, and I figure it will be fun and I am keen for an adventure. Although it's quite a distance, the course isn't too hilly, so it feels achievable.

Classic Ride 125km—QOM (Queen of the Mountain): "I can, I will—end of story." I quite like the saying that's on my gloves, it gives me a boost when I'm struggling.

I have fueled sufficiently, having enjoyed a big dinner with everyone at the house; I have my snacks in my pockets, and with everyone at the start line waiting to set off I share that I'm happy to go at my own pace, allowing others to push themselves. Hopefully see them at the rest stops, if not definitely at the end.

What a buzz, music playing we creep forward, groups of riders setting off at intervals. Fortunately, it's a nice day and I feel good. I lose everyone after about the first ten kilometres and I smile, actually chuckle to myself—see ya. No need to push and blow out as I've a distance to go and I'm finishing. I pace myself nicely and enjoy the ride.

Loads of time to be with my thoughts and appreciate my strong mind and body, as I cycle along the open road enjoying the scenery of Mudgee.

First stop for me is at sixty-five kilometres, I need to pee. Thankfully my friend Margot is looking out for me and takes my bike to rack it whilst I hurriedly make my way to the facilities. Grabbing a muesli bar and downing a vegemite sandwich, we set out, me trying to hold on to Margot and the group in front, but with no luck. I was happy to be out cycling, so again I relax back into my own pace.

Ninety-five kilometres is the next stop, and again Margot is there waiting, I use the facilities, refill my water and eat some more, and again we're on our way.

It's nice to stick together for the next twenty kilometres, I push a bit more knowing the end is near and we are sitting amongst a strong peloton of riders.

I cross the finish line, albeit solo, now—125 kilometres DONE! I hear my name being called out, and I smile, proud of myself. Not that I ever thought I wouldn't finish, but some days you just never know what the body can throw at you. It's wonderful to receive so many congratulations from my cycling club mates as we all come together, have a beverage and celebrate at the finish.

I'm quite drained and I don't hang around too long, as the adrenaline and buzz soon wears off. So I head home for a shower and to relax. It's definitely taken its toll on me, as I expected.

It's weird, once I conquer these goals I don't think too much about them until I have an 'off' day or I am being hard on myself.

Kicking Goals

Some days I just know there's no way I can do fifty kilometres, never mind 125 kilometres. But I love, value, and appreciate my tenacity and the drive to challenge myself and keep pushing, while allowing my body to rest and regenerate on those off days.

Back to reality after a few days, I continue conversations with my psychologist working on my insecurities and challenging the voices in my head. Accident or no accident these things are not unique to my situation. With guidance and support it's helpful to work through what holds us back or impacts our life, including our relationships. I share some of these thoughts and feelings with Adrian and the fact he listens, acknowledges them, and is okay with them makes me feel comfortable in my own skin and with our relationship.

Having the uncomfortable and often tough conversation never gets easier as it seems to rear its ugly head wherever I am in life. Putting thought to my approach, to the action, or the conversation is a must, as I find a more considered approach assists with shifting the discomfort. Always come from a place of kindness, knowing you're doing your best.

My third anniversary nears. I don't realise that my annual catch up with Mum falls on this day. Mother's Day is particularly special this year, not only are Mum and I together in the same state, but it is three years and one day since my accident. The day my brother showed up at her school classroom to tell her I had been hit by a car whilst cycling, and that I was in hospital unconscious, and in ICU on a ventilator.

The unwritten silence between a mother and daughter; neither of us speak much about my accident that day, we don't dwell on it, instead we choose to celebrate that we are together. This is particularly brave of my mother who went through so much too, her heartbreak of seeing me suffer is something I can never change, but I will always wish I could take it from her. To enjoy valuable time together, to see her smile and be proud of me every day as I keep moving forwards and live my life feels wonderful. Oh, and she is delighted meeting Adrian.

Mum always says she can tell a good person by their eyes—guess who has lovely eyes? Adrian!

Mums just want to hang with their daughters, and I will always cherish this simple joy that we share.

Where Am I Now?

My twelve-month journey writing this book and reliving what happened to me has provided me an enormous sense of achievement. My WHY is what has driven me: wanting to capture my story—inclusive of my struggles, heartache, key learnings and, of course, achievements—to provide hope for others.

It's quite surreal—me, Kelly-Anne, overcoming such adversity.

There were crashing waves of emotions as I wrote this book, triggering responses within my body—that still holds on to the trauma—which surprised me. My psychologist continually helps me to process a variety of feelings that, although I'm quite self-aware, uncover whatever is bubbling under the surface. We can't control everything, but we can work on creating positives, or tools, to replace negative thought patterns with healthier ones. Whether triggered by life, exhaustion, change, anxiety, or any combination of things, tuning in to my body is so important: allowing the space to be, to process, to breathe, and calm my nervous system. Noise-cancelling headphones are still a regular strategy I use to cut out external noise, to play meditative tunes to calm me, and to provide an escape when needed.

I end up resigning from my job, another tough decision, acknowledging it was doing more harm than good to my mental wellbeing. It wasn't right for me anymore.

I received final closure settling outside of court, the whole legal process had been completely draining for me. Once it was settled, a big sense of heaviness shifted for me. Now I have clarity on what my financial future looks like, I'm no longer dealing with lawyers, nor am I at the mercy of the insurance company. It's been over three years of constantly wondering and anticipating what might happen, the anxiety and uneasiness of so many unknowns were all out of my control. The constant juggling of so many variables, and trying to focus on my physical rehab, whilst barely coping with my mental anguish, was tough.

I continue to work with my psychologist, albeit not as frequently now, and this provides me with clarity and a comforting perspective on things. It keeps me accountable, and although some of the mental stuff has shifted my life will be forever impacted.

A new vocational consultant stirred a renewed sense of excitement within me, completing a deep-dive into my strengths, motivators, and future purpose. I loved that my thinking was challenged, and this resulted in a vision of POSSIBILITY with guidance and actions to work towards. I went from suffering from a lack of motivation to retain my pre-injury role, and struggling with my self-confidence post-accident, to now finding comfort in my renewed sense of purpose, and how I hope to help others on the horizon. Feeling heard and understood has made all the difference.

Being sent suggestions of courses I'm actually interested in, and which align with future career opportunities, has tested out old skills I hadn't had an opportunity to use since my accident. It's daunting, but exciting, moving forwards and simply trying whilst navigating the unknown. The impacts of my TBI are improving, and writing this book has been a catalyst for me to concentrate on, and think about, sentence construction as I articulate my story.

Where Am I Now?

I'm confident my life will continue to improve; it is unlikely that this will be without challenges, but I will deal with them as I have everything else: T E N A C I O U S L Y !

My new normal is pretty good, I work hard and I am moving towards a positive place of acceptance. My accident has definitely changed me, my values, what and who I give my energy to, and how I live my life. I'm constantly learning and rebuilding every aspect of it.

The person staring back at me in the mirror today is a strong, courageous, brave, determined, resilient and kind woman.

My Hero Skills are serving me well.

My injuries are mostly invisible now, which brings about a new set of challenges, as people think I'm okay when often I am not. Yet I try to get on with enjoying life, whilst being grateful and proud of all I am achieving.

I continue to work hard at the gym, and manage chronic pain, fatigue, and my overall wellbeing. There are things I can't control, but I do my best to work through them and focus on what I *can* control in order to remain positive.

Looking back, I realise the enormity of the lessons I learnt about myself, strengths I never realised I had, and my enormous growth over this three-year period, which continues as my recovery remains a constant in my life.

Exercising patience with myself, others, and external factors was a major learning curve and it proves to be a powerful trait, which I cherish.

Although I lost a piece of me, I've worked relentlessly to rebuild a new normal and I'm pretty happy with who I'm becoming. I'm a survivor, I'm here for a reason.

> *'You never know how strong you are until being strong is your only choice.'*
>
> Bob Marley

Hopefully I have inspired you, influenced your thinking, even *changed* your thinking, enabling you to look and move forwards.

So, I ask you ...

How are you going to embrace HOPE today?

Go out and live your best life.

Always remember the adage *'never judge a book by its cover'* because you don't know what's going on for people, disability or no disability. The *unseen* is as important as the *seen*.

Tell someone you love them, that you are grateful they are in your life. Smile to a stranger, you may just make their day. 😊

We can do amazing things if we just try, that's where it all begins, look forward and just try. Take that first step.

Stoicism is a gift. Here's to a flourishing life!

#dowhatyoulove

About The Author

Kelly-Anne Kerley was always destined to be a high achiever. Her relentless drive and desire to excel led her to leave her hometown of Adelaide in her early twenties, setting her sights on a corporate career in Sydney. Through hard work and determination she climbed the ranks, ultimately achieving a senior leadership role with a multinational corporation.

However, it was her love for road cycling that truly reflected her passion for physical and mental fitness. This love became crucial in her life after she endured a serious and traumatic collision with a car. Living with an incomplete Spinal Cord Injury (SCI), Traumatic Brain Injury (TBI), and other injuries, Kelly-Anne faced a daunting new reality. Yet, with unwavering resilience and determination she transformed hopelessness into hopefulness, altering her mindset and overcoming the challenges of her injuries.

Now residing in Sydney, Australia, with her partner Adrian, she has embraced her 'new normal.' As an avid cyclist once more, Kelly-Anne channels her experiences into a mission to educate, inspire, and empower others. She is passionate about sharing the wisdom she has gained to help people reshape their narratives and hold onto hope in the face of adversity.

Acknowledgements

This book would not have come to fruition without the support, encouragement, and guidance of several genuinely exceptional people.

To my mother, Lorraine, for diligently being by my side in hospital, for the home-cooked meals, to doing squats in physio and generally for being my ROCK. Thank you for your unwavering strength, support, and constant listening ear.

To my best friend, Carla, for always being there for me and for your never-ending kindness and love. I treasure our friendship every day, so grateful—you're sunshine for my soul.

To Jacqui and my cycling community, your support and encouragement kept me going and helped me to achieve my cycling goals, even when they felt out of reach. Your ongoing support of me and my cycling goals continues to this day.

To Bex Smith for recommending I enrol in Authorpreneurs Bootcamp at Disruptive Publishing, and for always being my cheerleader.

To Forward Ability Support (FAS—previously known as ParaQuad NSW), without their monetary support I would never have enrolled in Authorpreneurs Bootcamp and started my journey as a published author.

To John Maclean, Motivational Speaker, Author and Paralympian for writing the foreword to this book. John's book, *How Far Can You Go?*, about his own journey and quest to walk again after twenty-five years in a wheelchair, provided me with inspiration and the understanding that anything is possible.

To Brad Amos for skilfully capturing the perfect shot of me with my bike in front of a beautiful sunrise. This was only possible because of your passion for photography, and your gentle and kind nature.

To Andy Cooke, thank you for generously utilising your creative talents to craft the front and back covers. You have supported my message of *Hope* by bringing my story to life 'on the page'.

To my publisher Deborah Fay, and all the team at Disruptive Publishing for their expertise and guidance, and for helping me to turn my manuscript into a book.

To my editor, Jo Scott for actively preserving my voice and for making my editing experience an exciting journey of support and encouragement while bringing it all together

And finally, to all the dedicated health professionals (doctors, surgeons, specialists, nurses, therapists and more) who picked up the broken pieces after my accident and put me back together so that I could discover my new normal.

Cultivating 'Positive Mental Health' in Adults and Kids

Part of the proceeds from the purchase of each copy of *Breaking Up With My Wheelchair* will be donated to the BE **UNSTOPPABLE** Foundation

'HOLD ONTO HOPE
for your future is a canvas
waiting for your bright colours'

BE **UNSTOPPABLE** offers targeted programs to assist all people to manage stress and anxiety, overcome depression, strengthen their mindset, control their emotions, build resilience, build self-significance and find meaning in their life.

GIVING BACK AND CHANGING LIVES
Through coaching, counselling, compassion, empathy

Visit the BE **UNSTOPPABLE** website for support for your mental wellbeing, and to learn new management strategies to maintain better mental health.

www.beunstoppablefoundation.org

Your generosity is needed. Please support this charity.
Eligible gift donations are tax deductible.

Contact Kelly-Anne

 kellyannekerley.com

 kkerley1@hotmail.com

 https://www.linkedin.com/in/kellyannekerley/

It's a strong bond between me and my bike.
It's that intense feeling of total freedom and control.
It's so much more than just cycling, it's therapeutic.
My legs and bike make sure I go wherever I want to,
and my mind fills itself with great new memories.
At times it's tough, but in the end it's always worth it.

This is who I am.

I am a cyclist.

— Author unknown

Resources

BE UNSTOPPABLE FOUNDATION
Cultivating 'Positive Mental Health' in Adults and Kids
https://www.beunstoppablefoundation.org/

FORWARD ABILITY SUPPORT (FAS)
Supporting people with spinal cord injury to live their best life.
https://fas.org.au/

www.ingramcontent.com/pod-product-compliance
Lightning Source LLC
Chambersburg PA
CBHW061736070526
44585CB00024B/2700